FROM BURNOUT TO BELONGING

DISCOVER THE 5 MICROCULTURES THAT LEAD TO A LOW-STRESS WORKPLACE

KIMBERLY CAROZZI

KCAROZZI@HEALTHYHIVEPUB.COM

CONTENTS

ABOUT THE AUTHOR

Kimberly M. Carozzi spent years in the corporate world after earning her BS in Managerial Economics and her MBA in Marketing. After climbing the corporate ladder to work as an Operations Manager for a Fortune 100 company, Dr. Carozzi began to truly understand the problem, and prevalence, of burnout. After some soul searching, she went back to school as an adult to train as a chiropractor. A working mother, she personally understands the issues and problems resulting from stress/burnout from a corporate, managerial, and personal standpoint. She came across and used particular strategies to successfully change careers and create a work environment where employees could thrive and be happy in the workplace. Now, she wants to help others find relief and peace.

Dr. Carozzi is currently a practicing chiropractor and owns her own healthcare company.

THANK YOU FOR YOUR PURCHASE!

Scan the QR code below
*to receive your **FREE** Interview Checklist*
*and the **Burnout to Belonging Journal Pages** to get the most out*
of our content and begin your journey to low-stress work!

INTRODUCTION

"Burnout" is a syndrome resulting from chronic workplace stress that has not been successfully managed. Three dimensions characterize it:

- feelings of energy depletion or exhaustion;
- increased mental distance from one's job, or feelings of negativism or cynicism related to one's position; and
- reduced professional efficacy.

Burnout refers specifically to phenomena in the occupational context and should not be applied to describe experiences in other areas of life" (World Health Organization, 2019).

Burnout comes in many forms, though we don't often recognize it. The mental symptoms are easiest to recognize: brain fog, forgetfulness, low mood, irritability, and a loss of interest. When we think of burnout, the mental side is what we think about. The physical symptoms are forgotten about, written off. We pop a painkiller and keep moving forward, making the problem worse.

In my time as a chiropractor, I have encountered patients with back problems from chronic work-related stress. The body is an efficient machine, and it signals when something is wrong.

A fluttering eyelid, a headache, a stiff neck, and lower back pain. These are all physical symptoms of burnout, and we need to pay attention to them. However, "curing" burnout is not always the best course of action. Instead, we should keep in mind the old saying that prevention is better than cure. Rather than taking acetaminophen for a headache and using up our PTO just to get some space from work, we need to take a moment to reflect on the situation that's causing us to feel burned out.

Burnout can be challenging to treat. The typical treatments are restful sleep, spending time with loved ones, and getting a little physical activity each day. However, the mere effort of trying to do these things can cause further stress. Once again, it's best to identify the root of the problem: you are stressed. So chronically stressed that your body is starting to respond negatively. Many things can cause workplace stress.

Perhaps you had a disagreement with a coworker, and working together causes you stress. You might have been handed a complex case to complete and are having trouble finding the time. Or you're working from home and are struggling to separate your workspace from your home life.

Everybody has felt and will feel burnout. It's inevitable. Even self-help gurus like Tony Robbins and Brené Brown have been burned out. The problem with burnout is that it starts small. You start by wanting to make a good impression—to please your boss and coworkers. You want to prove how dedicated you are, so you take on more than you can handle.

And most importantly, you want to prove to yourself your own worth. The COVID-19 pandemic restrictions also haven't been helpful. Where some people thrived working from home, others had difficulty adjusting because they missed the sociability of the workplace. Humans are social creatures; we weren't made for the isolation of four walls and a desk.

This leads to the most severe problem caused by burnout: you don't feel good enough. You begin to feel absent and disconnected like you don't deserve to move up or enjoy your career. All the self-help blogs you read feel like they're giving you false hope. You feel like you'll never have your own success story, that the roadmap out of the mire doesn't exist for you.

And that's why I'm here: to give you the roadmap. Throughout this book, I'm going to help you conquer your work stress and defeat your burnout. I will show you that you are, in fact, good enough and worth more than just your job title. In the chapters defining the five microcultures, you will find "journaling questions." This is to give you a chance to think about the office culture you're working in. You might find specific quirks of the Classroom microculture within your current workplace, or the Kingdom in a past workplace. That's part of the roadmap, and it will help you decide whether you want to stay and change the way you're working, or if you want to seek out a new career with a microculture where you can thrive.

1

THE "OLD-FASHIONED" MODEL OF CAREER SUCCESS

Failure is simply the opportunity to begin again, this time more intelligently.

— HENRY FORD

Burnout is a tricky topic to address. It's been around for a very long time, and it's only recently that we've started to truly understand it. The traditional career model has its roots in the aftermath of World War Two. At this time, people were not only struggling from the Great Depression, but the world had literally been at war for close to five years. There needed to be a model in place to help people survive and prosper. This is where the traditional career model comes in. While that worked for a time, with the onset of the Technological Revolution, which saw the birth of commercial computers and the Internet, it began to unravel.

Just like the Industrial Revolution revolutionized the world, the Technological Revolution revolutionized the workplace. Thus began the downfall of the traditional career model, which rapidly became outdated. The traditional model relies on choosing your career based on your personality. For example, a career aptitude test might tell you you'll make a great teacher because you're gregarious. These tests match your personality to specific skill sets and inventories. However, there is one big problem with this model: it doesn't consider the work sphere or environment.

Although you might be working a job you match with, you are experiencing burnout because your workplace doesn't fit your individual needs. We all deserve to have our needs met at work, just like we deserve to have our needs met in our personal lives. That could mean asking for an extension to complete your work or asking for compressed hours to free up an extra day or afternoon. If these needs aren't being met, it can and will prevent you from achieving the success you desire.

The Traditional Career Model

We all grew up with the traditional career model, and we are now starting to see how flawed it is. It all starts with grouping our personalities into skill sets. A creative personality excels at abstract thinking, a logical personality excels at team management, and so on. These skill sets are applied to suitable career paths, which leads to a career search and our choice of profession. The creative personality may seek graphic design, the logical personality might pursue engineering. We then train for a degree or other qualification and get a job in that profession. When we train in our chosen profession, we have been trained to help clients, customers, our bosses, and our coworkers. We deliver our services, get rewarded, and in theory, we enjoy the career we have chosen.

But that doesn't always happen.

When it doesn't happen, when we aren't rewarded or the rewards stop coming, we work even harder. As we work even harder, we expect the rewards to return, and when that doesn't happen, burnout starts to set in.

According to a 2012 report by Net Impact, it's evident that what employees desire from work has changed since the aftermath of World War Two. While the post-World War Two generation wanted security and stability, today's younger generations want career fulfillment, a positive environment, and a good work/life balance (Net Impact, 2012). It could be said that we are better skilled at career management in the 21st Century than ever before. In fact, it's still a pretty new area of study and training. Perhaps this is why the traditional career model is no longer viable.

Why the Traditional Career Model Doesn't Work

One of the problems with the traditional career model is that it doesn't incorporate microcultures. As a result, modern professionals are unable to assess or recognize the microculture which best serves them. In plain terms, a microculture is a small group of people who share particular interests and have their own way of communication or working. It's difficult to understand a company's microculture just by looking at their mission statement or the organization's beliefs. A microculture depends on the interplay among managers and employees, and as a result, this dictates what they encounter beyond their work tasks.

Therein lies the link: your needs versus what your job is offering you. Once you understand this link, you can better understand the nature of your burnout, and take the appropriate steps to get rid of your symptoms. You could be working in your dream career, with incredible people, but if your job and managers aren't offering anything in return, it might be time to reassess if this is the microculture you want. According to the traditional career model, the type of job and work matter more than the microculture. I propose the opposite. The job and work do not matter as much when you're trying to work out how well the worker will fit in with their job.

Finding where you fit could be the key to overcoming your burnout. Most often, the option to simply leave your job and seek greener pastures is not the wisest course of action. I was fortunate enough to be in a position to retrain in a field of my choice, and that's something not everyone has access to. You might not be ready or able to leave your current position. There are still things you can do to overcome the burnout you're currently facing. One of them is recognizing your company's current microculture, and playing within it. This recognition will give you the tools you need to function and survive while you find where you feel you truly belong.

FROM MARKETING TO HEALTHCARE

As I said, not everyone is in the position I was when I retrained. If it's an option for you, I suggest you take it. Nothing gives you such a feeling of control like taking command of your own career. If you're not in the position to do that yet, keep holding on. Your time will come, of that you can be certain. I feel that my story is relevant in both situations. We all grew up with the same narrative: follow the traditional career model and you will succeed! I think the last couple of decades have taught us that that's not always the case. Usually, it's the outliers who find the most fulfillment, even if it's not financial success. With that in mind, I'm not here to tell you how to achieve financial success (that's for another book). I'm here to tell you how to overcome your burnout, and find a sense of belonging.

Before I discovered my passion for chiropractic, I worked for a Fortune 100 company. More specifically, I was an Operations Manager. I went to school for the job, eventually earning a BS in Managerial Economics and an MBA in Marketing. It was a lot of work and late nights studying, but upon my MBA graduation, I was thrilled and proud of everything I had achieved. When I worked my way up to Operations Manager, I should have felt like Queen of the World. But was I happy? In theory, yes, I didn't have anything to complain about. In reality, I was taking work home with me, I was exhausted, and a good night's sleep just wasn't working for me the way it should have. The company I worked for was voted "Best Workplace in America," but I wasn't feeling it.

My answer was a complete change in career paths. Going back to school as an adult is contrary to the traditional career model. You go to school as a child and teenager, train as a young adult, and what you train for is what you do for the rest of your life. It was nerve-racking to think I'd be the oldest person in the classroom. What I found was that I wasn't the oldest. In fact, there were several men and women around my age, some who were younger, but overall, I didn't feel out of place. Once I completed my training, I was a fully-fledged chiropractor. That doesn't mean I don't use my previous training. In fact, it helped me found my own healthcare company. Although the work is its own brand of tiring, I'm not burned out. This is because I have the opportunity to create my own microculture.

Occupational burnout is a byproduct of the outdated traditional career model. It manifests in corporate and managerial professions, and can be difficult to manage. The strategies I'm sharing in this book I had to come across on my own, and I have chosen to share them with you, because I know what it's like to feel empty, isolated, and like I'm stuck in a career that was chosen for me by a career aptitude test. If you find that a career change is also your answer, you will find a roadmap to a career change in these pages. Or you might find that you're stuck at the bottom of the ladder in a job you like. I hope to help you find a way to the next rung, and the one above that. I want you to be happy in your workplace, wherever that may be.

WHY TRADITIONAL EMPLOYMENT IS OBSOLETE

Traditional employment, and the traditional career model, both served their purpose for a couple of decades. Then, following a series of stock market crashes, some depressions, a little austerity here and there, plus the skyrocketing cost of living and a global pandemic, it suddenly stopped being relevant. We cannot ignore the role the pandemic played in the evolution of employment. Remote working, in jobs which were previously "impossible to make remote," was suddenly an option. Greater flexibility was now available to a lot of us. It also spurred the growth of an entirely new economy.

You may have heard the term "gig economy." A gig economy is defined by the rise in people who take on short term contracts or freelance work in place of permanent jobs. Although gig work has been around for decades, we are seeing the rise of people who make their living through flexible work. This could be through picking up jobs on apps like TaskRabbit, or it could be by owning your own freelance company. Gig work is multifaceted and relies on both skilled and unskilled labor. While a 9-to-5 job might suit some people, others find freedom in working regular gigs.

One of the reasons traditional employment is becoming obsolete is the common complaint of commuting. At present, we still accept the idea of a 9-to-5, eight-hour workday. Not too long ago, the 8/8/8 rule of time division was accepted. This meant "eight hours of work, eight hours of rest, eight hours of leisure" as a standard way of viewing the 24-hour period of a day. However, there are problems with this, and they are related to commuting. If you work eight hours a day, five days a week, that doesn't include the time you spend traveling to and from work. Assuming it's an hour each way, that's two hours unaccounted for, and they have to come from somewhere. They usually come from your rest and relaxation time. For this reason, companies have begun to experiment with compressed hours. For example, you might leave at 1 pm on a Friday if you add two hours each to your Monday and Wednesday. Another reason is that transport infrastructures are struggling to keep up with the increased load of people who are commuting to and from work. The reason it's called "rush hour" is because people are rushing to get home, leading to heavy traffic and longer commuting times.

As the internet became more refined and we harnessed its powers to our benefit, the digital economy began to boom. This led to a rise in entrepreneurship and online businesses. Easy access to large global markets and resources helped businesses grow, and today we are seeing more startups and new businesses spring up. People began to take control of their working life. As a result, there was an increase in productivity and job fulfillment to such an extent that the traditional job market began to look less appealing. Working from home was a thing long before the 2020 lockdowns because so many businesses can be run from your laptop or the comfort of your bed. Why work for someone else when you can work for yourself?

Journaling Questions:

- Do you notice any similarities between your current or past work experience and the traditional career model?
- What aspects of the old career model do you feel have worked well for you? Which aspects do you feel have worked against you or made it harder for you to achieve "success"?

Workplaces are slowly adjusting to create a hybrid model that seeks to embrace both the traditional and new ways of working. However, during this transition period, some of the traditional myths about work still persist. These myths are often to blame for the differences in viewpoint, which result in misunderstanding and the resultant burnout that occurs as people try to prove themselves worthy of the requirements that the workplace has placed on them. In the next chapter, we will look at some of these workplace myths that have guided our workplaces and careers for so long.

2

THE TOP WORKPLACE "MYTHS" OF EFFECTIVE PERSON-CULTURE FIT

An unfortunate byproduct of the traditional career model is the sheer amount of workplace myths that have accumulated. Some of us have grown up with the post-industrial idea that "work is work, work is life," or we view what we do for a job as what we will do for the rest of our natural-born lives. Consequently, we take the view that we aren't allowed to enjoy our time off, we make a point of not using our PTO, or take artificial pride in working exorbitant amounts of overtime. While having some extra money might be helpful, if we think that not taking a sick day shows dedication to the company, the fact remains that we are putting ourselves last in favor of work. All of this compounds into a series of workplace "myths" which need to be busted.

COMMON WORKPLACE MYTHS

Over the years, as the traditional career model evolved, a collection of workplace myths began to crop up. You might have heard your 50-something aunt or uncle, or your older coworkers, complain that "kids these days just don't want to work" and felt a touch of annoyance at the accusation that you're lazy. You may have also seen an Instagram influencer brag about how much money they make and share their secrets, promoting "the grind." Not everybody wants to grind for a living. Some of us just want our days off to be our days off. The five listed below are only a handful of the myths which have sprung up. If you can think of any more, you can write them down as part of your reflection at the end of this chapter.

Myth One: Longer Hours Means Higher Productivity

This is an old-school way of thinking. It posits that working longer means you are able to get more done. While, in theory, this should mean more time to complete your tasks and any extra, it actually means more energy expended. You might find that employees like to boast about how many hours they work and how it means that they're incredibly hard working. You might work a six-hour shift while another person works for nine hours. That doesn't mean that you are any less tired on the six-hour shift, because you might have had to wake up earlier, or take a longer commute to get to work, or you're working more hours overall that week. The person on the nine-hour shift is working longer, but they might thrive under longer hours. The length of your shift does not matter. In both cases, both employees could be working even longer hours. While an employer will look at this as an opportunity for increased productivity, what's actually happening is the employees are getting tired more quickly. As a result, work quality and output both suffer.

Casey works in education. She enjoys it. The hours are stable, the work is manageable, and she loves working with kids. However, the workday doesn't stop when the bell rings. She has a mountain of homework waiting for her when she gets home. Essays to grade, tests to mark, and she doesn't know how any of it will help her students. While everyone tells her that her job must be super easy because she doesn't work the hours they do in customer service, she's quietly stewing because, for her, the workday almost never ends. She has conferences and training sessions to attend in addition to grading homework, and her last real "day off" feels as if it were an eternity ago. As a result, her students' papers aren't graded until weeks after they're handed in, she can't focus during the conferences, and her mind wanders while she assigns her students "silent reading time." Her productivity is not what it was when she first got into teaching.

Myth 2: Money Is the Best Motivation

"Money makes the world go around" sings the M.C. in Kander and Ebb's *Cabaret*. Although this is true to an extent, on a more personal level, money is not the only source of motivation. I don't blame you if you grew up with the idea of the almighty dollar as the sole source of motivation. You might have grown up in poverty, and a high-paying career was ingrained in you as the only viable way out. In today's culture, success and net worth are deeply intertwined. Research has shown that people are motivated by more than just money. Indeed, motivation itself is more complicated than just the numbers in your bank account. Fulfillment and meaning are just two of the intrinsic and intangible factors that support a person's motivation. Something tangible like money might be a way to measure your job performance, but your own sense of belonging might be more important to you.

Jonathan works as a barista for a well-known chain of coffee shops. He enjoys the work, and he likes talking to customers. Customers love him, and he gets a lot of physical activity in, which is good because he plays soccer with his friends on a Sunday. However, despite being clear on his availability, Jonathan's boss, Sarah, keeps putting him down for longer hours. Having been with the company for a few years, he hasn't seen his pay increase. It has remained at the same level it was when he first started, and the cost of living keeps going up. While Jonathan is grateful for the extra hours and the money they bring, his job is only a part of his life. He has friends and hobbies which he would love to make time for, but he's always working. Soon, he begins to lose all motivation to do his job to the high standard that he's always performed.

Does this scenario sound familiar? It's all too common and lays the foundation for burnout.

Myth 3: People Don't Want to Work Hard

While it may seem like people don't like working, the truth is many employees are simply "disengaged" from their work. Basically, they aren't thrilled about the job itself, and consequently aren't enthusiastic about showing up to work. This could be due to any number of reasons, including:

- A bad boss
- A lack of a clear vision
- No form of recognition
- Layers of bureaucracy that get in the way of progress
- Lack of challenge on the job
- A mismatch between the job requirements and the employee's inherent strengths and talents

Or, it could be a combination of any of the above. You might not be as motivated to perform as you did when you were new to the job. What others think of as laziness is actually a disengagement from a position that doesn't appreciate you. Ultimately, it's not so much a characterization of your work ethic as it is an indication that the nature of your job, as well as external factors, don't mesh well with your needs.

Alex always wanted to work in tech. He was gifted in math and science when he was a child, and his first job in programming with a major tech company turned into a career. Alex worked incredibly hard during the first couple of years, but as time went on, things in the company just didn't feel right. His manager changed multiple times, so Alex, the good soldier that he was, hunkered down and made sure the train stayed on the tracks, and all of the work got done. Despite the office climate, Alex was a stable and productive professional and he made sure that his department performed well. After several supervisory changes, Alex lost sight of what he enjoyed about his work. Sure, he was good at it, but where was the challenge? Alex soon realized that just because he was good at something, that didn't necessarily mean that that's what he wanted to do every day. So, he started asking for more challenges and an opportunity to manage. Responsibilities were happily handed over, but the promotion never came. One Alex realized he was wasting his time and effort, the pressure of overwork began taking its toll, and he felt his only solution was to leave the company.

Myth 4: Managers Are Willing and Able to Change the Work Environment

Many employees are often scared that if they speak up about issues and problems that are important to them, they will run the risk of being shunned or seen as a "problem employee." This is particularly true in the context of a corporate job. There's a certain hierarchy in a corporate job that can leave newer employees feeling intimidated and unseen. Depending on the priorities of upper management and their leadership style, middle and entry-level managers may recognize problems in the workplace but lack the authority to fix them. It may be surprising to employees to realize that their managers, too, must tread carefully when suggesting change or pointing out problems. They can be viewed as an impediment to "achieving the company's mission" and ineffective at their job. Upper management may perceive "problems" as an attack on their abilities and lack of support for company goals. In some cases, confidential hotlines exist to report illegal or harassing behavior, but the reaction and response to these reports may not be evident right away. When sensitive matters are handled behind the scenes by the human resources department or upper management, the "reporter" won't know what, if any action has been taken. Fortunately, many workplace cultures are designed so that employees don't incur penalties simply because they want to discuss what they feel are inadequacies in the work environment. Keep your suggestions process oriented, and not personal, although it may be tempting to do so. In any case, if you do choose to air your concerns and are met with resistance, this a sign that your workplace may not be a good fit for you.

Marissa hated her job. The work was fine, she was capable of doing it, but the company culture was the worst. She thought she had friends at work, but she later found out they were using the ideas she shared with them to get ahead. They made suggestions to upper management about cost-saving ideas and took the credit. When she told her manager about what she was going through, she was advised to "go to therapy" and "keep to herself" because "that's just how business is." Her manager even confided that she was also actively interviewing for a transfer to another department. Marissa was devastated by the behavior of her colleagues, and she was so upset she began having migraines from stress and lack of sleep. Even her therapist advised her to seek a company culture she could work with, with a manager who was willing and able to help her feel comfortable and safe in her work environment. Marissa, once a friendly and engaged employee, began to withdraw, and do the minimum necessary to keep her job.

Myth 5: Having Fun Is Bad for Productivity

One of the biggest misconceptions about the nature of work and the workplace is that you can only get things done if you take a completely stoic and serious attitude to your work. You aren't allowed to have colleagues you get along with or be distracted by the breakroom conversations about the latest hit TV show. Instead, your mind must be focused on the job every second of the workday, and all friendly conversations must be saved for private chats because they are seen as a waste of precious work time. This couldn't be further from the truth. The problem with making the workplace a fun-free zone is that employees can often become depressed and excessively stressed, leading to poor performance on the job. Having friends at work can be encouraging because it means you enjoy being around those people. Work environments where you feel like you're part of a team and aren't just there to get paid and go home are great for productivity. There's an element of trust in workplace friendships, which makes delegating tasks much easier. Having a fun work environment helps encourage employee engagement, which in turn can help boost job productivity.

Daniel's office recently got a new manager. His old manager was a laid-back woman who felt like she was everyone's mother. She always took care of everyone and took action when there was trouble. When she was transferred to a new location, Daniel's team was ready for the newest member of their little family. What they got was a manager who refused to participate in the team dynamic. He frequently refused invitations to events and shouted down anyone who was seen to be having fun. Things at Daniel's workplace quickly soured. Although productivity looked to be doing well, it was nowhere near the same level as it had been under Daniel's old manager.

Journaling Questions:

- Do any of these workplace myths resonate with you?
- What are some workplace myths you've come to realize are false?

Some workplaces which still rely on the traditional career model also rely on some commonplace myths about company culture. These bosses believe that offering more money will improve their employees' productivity when we know this is not always the case. It's also commonly thought that people don't want to work hard, which you know is untrue. You work incredibly hard at a job that will replace you within moments of your resignation.

Now that we've debunked many of the mainstream myths when it comes to workplace culture, let's talk about how to recognize when you're burning out.

3

10 SIGNS YOU'RE BURNING OUT

"A light that burns twice as bright burns half as long."

— DR. ELDON TYRELL (BLADE RUNNER)

Y ou don't have to work a high-profile career to be burned out. I know firsthand that you can work a career you dreamed about all your life, and still burn out. It's true that some industries are more stressful than others, but the type and hours of work can be equally demanding. Working on a construction crew is more labor-intensive than working as an Operations Manager for a Fortune 100 company, but both have their own demands. Heavy labor is physically exhausting while the Operations Manager role demands more mental energy. At the end of the day, both types of work can leave you drained, whether you enjoy it or not.

WHAT IS BURNOUT?

"Burnout" is not a medical diagnosis. Rather, it's a serious byproduct of stress specifically related to work. It's characterized by feeling physically and/or emotionally drained, and often associated with decreased sense of accomplishment and even a loss of your personal or professional identity. Although some people might regard burnout as an excuse to be lazy, it's a very real phenomenon. More people than you think struggle with it.

There are a few cues that could be an indication that you're experiencing burnout on the job. Here are a few questions you can ask yourself:

- Have you become increasingly cynical or critical on the job as of late?

This can come in many forms. Perhaps you're criticizing the new hire for not doing their job right. You might be criticizing yourself because, out of the thousand times you've done something right, you've done it wrong once. Or, you might be becoming disillusioned with your work life. Your attitude might have shifted from excited to start a new role in a new industry with new responsibilities, to feeling a sense of existential dread when you hear your morning alarm.

- Do you feel like you have to drag yourself to work and find it hard to do your job?

Fatigue and lack of motivation are common symptoms of burnout. Working in the wrong microculture can have this effect. When we work with people we can trust and have fun with, we thrive and are able to do our jobs to the best of our ability. However, when you don't fit with the microculture, it can be difficult to find your place. You feel like an outcast, a misfit, as though you don't belong there and like you have to persevere in the hope that things will eventually get better. They might get better later, but is it worth spending months or potentially years dragging yourself out of bed for a job that doesn't seem to want you?

- Do you act impatiently with the people you interact with at work?

Over time, our patience can grow thin. The workplace is no exception. You've been doing something for years and are fully capable, but someone who's new to the duties you're used to might take a little time learning them. In this case, losing a little patience is understandable. We're all familiar with that scene in every movie about a middle-aged man or woman having a midlife crisis: a lot of minor things happen, they build up, and eventually, the main character loses it and takes their rage out on the printer or their coworkers. This is how every burned-out employee *would like* to respond to their situation, but it's not right. If you feel like this is you, you might be burned out.

- Do you feel too exhausted to be regularly productive?

No matter how much sleep you get, or how restful it is, you always seem to feel exhausted. You might have a fun chat with the barista as you get your morning coffee, or you see a funny meme on Instagram, then when you walk into work, you're suddenly drained. Moving feels slow, speaking seems to take too much effort, and an hour passes in the space of 10 minutes. This begins to affect your work to the point where you do the absolute bare minimum, and your productivity slows down. The more your productivity suffers, the more punishments you get at work, the more you tell yourself, "It's fine," and the cycle continues.

- Is it difficult to concentrate?

Difficulty concentrating can happen across our personal and professional lives. We start a task; it goes well for a few minutes, then suddenly we lose interest. We turn on the television, get lost in a rerun, then we grab our phones and start scrolling through social media. A loss of concentration is your brain signaling to you that it's time for a change. That could be searching for a new job, beginning an entirely new career, or simply using some of the PTO you've accrued. Alternatively, it might be worth consulting a therapist or seeking other treatment.

- Do you notice a lack of satisfaction with your accomplishments?

Impostor syndrome is a psychological occurrence where you believe that you aren't as competent as others perceive you to be. For example, your boss tells you you've earned a raise, your coworkers come to you for help with something they know you're good at, and your productivity is the best in the office. On the outside, you're a model employee. On the inside, you hate yourself because you feel like a fraud. Impostor syndrome is usually accompanied by a deep sense of dissatisfaction with your accomplishments. You feel that you didn't work hard enough to earn them, or that you don't deserve to pursue your goals at all. When we're burned out, we gaslight ourselves into believing we don't deserve our accomplishments.

- Are you feeling disillusioned about your job?

Disillusionment is a sense that something isn't as good as you thought it would be. When we start a new career, we're excited. We're offered a lot of amazing benefits early on; we enjoy being the newbie, and we love learning on the job. Then, suddenly, it's been five years, and nothing seems to have changed. You get up, go to work, do your job, go home, go to bed. That becomes your routine, and you start to long for something more, and it's almost as if nothing matters anymore. We feel disillusioned because of the adrenaline rush that comes in the early stages of something new, and once it fades, it can feel like it's too late to make any changes. Disillusionment lifts when we decide to make active changes.

- Are you attempting to treat your feelings with food, drugs, or alcohol?

This is sneaky. We don't always recognize how our mood affects the way we cope. Alcohol is a depressant, which means it helps us relax. Certain substances such as marijuana can assist with that relaxed or buzzed feeling and eating foods we enjoy can give us a nice hit of serotonin or dopamine, the happiness and reward chemicals. However, this behavior is not healthy. Relying on food, drugs, and alcohol can lead to devastating consequences on your health. In particular, addiction. We come to rely on these substances in order to feel better about ourselves because, although our bosses and coworkers can talk back to us, the substances we use can't. If you are concerned you're misusing substances to cope with your burnout, please seek professional help.

- Have your sleep habits gotten worse?

This could go either way: either you sleep too little or too much. Remember what I said about feeling exhausted? No matter how much we sleep, we might always feel tired. Or, if you get too little sleep, you stress about needing to catch up, and that stress frustrates you to the extent that you can't sleep. It becomes a cycle. Stress affects our circadian rhythm because of the hormones involved: cortisol and adrenaline. Although these have their place in certain functions, when we're stressed, the constant production of cortisol and adrenaline keeps our brains wired in the "fight or flight" response.

- Are you affected by random headaches, stomach aches, or other types of physical illnesses?

The body keeps the score in more ways than one, and stress is no exception. Just like with your sleep habits, your body and brain are in "fight or flight" mode. As it's meant to be a short-term response inherited from our caveman ancestors to help us survive against predators, its place in the office is subject to debate. Consequently, the longer it goes on, the more pronounced its effect becomes. Stomach aches and gastrointestinal disruptions are common due to the increase of cortisol, while headaches can be a result of increased or decreased blood pressure. Our immunity also drops during periods of stress because the parasympathetic nervous system— "rest and digest"—is being overpowered by the sympathetic nervous system— "fight or flight." When this happens, it's time to acknowledge that something is wrong.

If any of these statements apply to you, then there's a possibility that you're experiencing job burnout. It's at this point that I would like to advise you to put the book down, make yourself a cup of tea or some hot chocolate, and simply rest. Admitting that you're burned out is a huge step, but once you've acknowledged it, it becomes easier to deal with. There are many options available to you. Not everyone chooses to go to therapy at first—it's an option I will always recommend—so you might choose to try yoga, meditation, changing your diet, or finding a creative or physical outlet. There are many ways to manage burnout and work-related stress. Burnout is not simply "feeling tired" or "being lazy," it's a symptom of a much larger problem.

THE PREVALENCE OF WORKPLACE BURNOUT

Burnout is much more common than we want to believe. Feeling despondent, depressed, fatigued, or otherwise hopeless at work are all common symptoms. If you're a manager, you probably think that your employees are lazy or unmotivated when you see these symptoms. *We all get tired,* you might be thinking, so you tell them, "You have to keep pushing!" If you're an employee, you're wondering what's wrong with you and why you can't seem to break out of it. You might ask for more challenging projects, only to find that

that makes the problem worse. Being given new responsibilities on top of all the work you already do might not be the best course of action, regardless of how well you plan your workload. No matter how well you plan your time and energy, there's only so much you can do.

Burnout is not just limited to your one particular office. It's a global phenomenon, and it took a pandemic and almost two years of remote working to recognize it. According to a survey by Deloitte, 77% of over 1000 respondents reported experiencing burnout at work. 83% reported that burnout was beginning to negatively affect their personal lives and relationships. These statistics also include 64% of people who reported enjoying their job, but also that stress at work was beginning to negatively affect their performance. Most shocking of all revelations from this one Deloitte survey found that, overall, employees feel that their employers simply aren't doing enough. Whether that's to prevent burnout or lift some of the workplace stressors that may be causing it, or somewhere in between, employees are feeling the burn.

We also cannot ignore the effects of the Covid-19 pandemic or 2020 itself. From January 2020, it seems like the world has been playing one long game of Jumanji, with each month representing a new challenge. As the pandemic progressed, people felt like personal freedoms were under threat. "Issues like the politicization of masks and vaccines and feelings of lack of support from the government and workplaces have caused workers—especially those in public-facing jobs—to become cynical about their jobs and about the public in general" (Abramson, 2022). While cynicism has its place in philosophy, as a worldview, it is quite exhausting. Workers began to feel like they were being undermined, and that they had no value in the workplace. They were, literally, bringing the workplace home with them in the form of remote working.

What Causes Job Burnout?

Job burnout is multifactorial, but it can be caused by just one consistent factor. Some people might become burned out by one problem which keeps repeating itself, which they're too resigned to speak up about. Others might be okay with one or two problems, but when the problems start to pile up, they can start to feel the strain. There are so many things that can lead to burnout that a list of them all would become its own book. Instead, for the purposes of this section, I am going to address the most common causes of burnout.

One of the most common causes of burnout is a lack of workplace autonomy. This means that you don't have enough freedom to dictate certain aspects of your job. For example, you might employ your own tricks when using Excel, which is more efficient than the company guidelines. Your managers might force you to do it the way the company demands, even if you find it more difficult. In theory, you know your job better than your managers, but you don't have the autonomy to do it as efficiently as you usually would.

Another cause for burnout is that although there's a description for your role, it's not always clear what's expected of you. Companies can expect "excellence" from you and that you will "go above and beyond" in the role, but those are very loose terms. Not knowing what standards you should be seeking to meet can leave you constantly second-guessing your performance in relation to what your manager expects of you.

Another reason for burnout could be poor workplace culture. A lot of companies like to brag about how their company is "like a little family," but the truth is that family doesn't always get along. Some teams might have a healthy dynamic, and others might completely ignore each other. You might thrive in an environment where you can get along with everyone, so the second culture would be detrimental for you. Conversely, you might prefer more independence, which would mean that a team with a social dynamic might make you uncomfortable. Everyone has the right to feel safe and comfortable in their workplace. Feeling uncomfortable in your work environment can also contribute to job burnout and stress.

A lack of social support might also leave you feeling stressed and burned out. While we're seeing a rise in prioritizing our personal lives over our professional lives, we're still beholden to the belief that putting work first means you're a hard worker. Humans are social creatures; I don't know how much clearer I can make that. Without a strong social network to rely on, it can be hard to find relief from work-related stress.

Consequently, this can lead to a work-life imbalance. Remember what I said about the "8/8/8 rule"? It's impossible to divide your day up like that because you will always have to compromise on either your rest or your leisure time. If your work starts to consume your everyday life, leaving you with little or no time to spend with the family, this can lead to burnout.

You're Blaming the Wrong Person

Going through burnout is tough for everyone. Sometimes, you may not even know you're suffering through it, only to wake up with a host of physical and mental health problems. A lot of times, the anxiety and stress we feel is self-imposed. It's because we don't feel we're good enough, and we worry that we're not performing to the best of our abilities. It's easy to blame ourselves for the anxiety we feel. However, sometimes, it's really nobody's fault for the way we feel when we're burned out. These things happen, and there's no reason to feel ashamed about feeling the way you do. At the end of the day, you can't always control how you end up feeling or how you or your body reacts to your environment and day-to-day life. Just know that there's hope ahead, and that you will soon be able to reignite your passion for life once again.

Why Burnout Can Actually Be a Good Thing

The surprising thing about burnout is that it's actually a signal—a signal that it's time to change. Burnout helps you change your perspective on your career and what your idea of success looks like. The truth is that it's experiences like burnout that help you become a stronger and more self-aware individual. When you experience burnout, it makes you think twice about what's important in life and forces you to prioritize the things in life that actually make you happy. This then allows you to separate society's goals and definitions of success from what you feel is the best definition and conception of success for you and what you want to achieve in your life. Ultimately, although burnout can be stressful in the moment and make you feel like the world is coming to an end, it can also be the tipping point you need to turn your life around and steer yourself toward the goals you truly want to achieve for yourself.

Hurry Fever

This is a uniquely American cultural trait. "Hurry Fever" is not an official medical diagnosis; rather it's a phenomenon. We start school young, and we focus on going from elementary school to middle school, then from middle school to high school, and from high school to college or trade school, and then straight to work. All we think about is the next thing. What comes next? Ultimately, it seems that the "last thing," the goal, is to land a job we spend years training for. Then we focus on the next promotion, and when it doesn't happen, we try to rush it. When we are not where we expect to be by some ambiguous standard, we feel a lack of accomplishment, and pressure ourselves to accomplish more and more. I have listened to teenagers express angst and frustration about not "knowing what they are going to do" with the rest of their life. Are we really equipped to answer this question at fourteen years old? Do we ever really know the one thing we are meant to do for the rest of our lives? What about discovery, change and evolution as we grow as human beings? We don't allow for these times of self-reflection as we rush to please parents, peers and teachers. This phenomenon sets the stage to just "get a job, any job" without consideration of what is best for mental health. All of this energy is spent on rushing from one stage to the next, and in between, we forget to live.

THE TRUE COST OF BURNOUT

In addition to your mental and physical health, burnout affects your personal and professional life. This can have severe implications on your team, and consequently, your business. However, there is one aspect of burnout nobody talks about: the true human cost of burnout. When you tell someone that you're stressed, they might say to you, "Try to relax" or "Do yoga" or "Change your diet." While those are all useful tips for addressing the symptom, it's not a cure for the cause. When the cause isn't dealt with, it can have a severe impact on your health.

To put this into perspective, burnout and stress-related illnesses lead to almost 120,000 deaths per year (Harvard Business Review, 2019). Additionally, the cumulative costs associated amount to nearly $190 billion per year (Harvard Business Review, 2019). Depression and anxiety affect people all over the world, to the extent that the World Health Organization estimates an almost $1 trillion loss of productivity each year. Depression also sees a cost of over $51 billion in lost productivity as well as absenteeism, including the burned-out employees who are more likely to take a day off (Mental Health America). It's common to hear in the world of business that depression is something you should just get over, and anxiety is just feeling nervous a lot of the time. With both of these conditions, you're expected to "just deal with it" or "get over it." While you can take steps to manage your mental health, I would like to reiterate my previous point: you can treat the symptom, but unless you cure the cause, it will keep plaguing you. In this context, it's unsurprising that burned-out employees are more likely to actively seek new employment (Wigert and Agrawal, 2018).

Most companies do not have protocols in place to alleviate employee burnout, which can negatively impact employee retention. Unresolved frustration, lack of job satisfaction, and a lack of engagement are all contributing factors to burnout. It is unfair to place the blame for burnout and stress on the employee when the employer, and company, have a responsibility to safeguard the health of their employees. This is why we are living in, and suffering the ongoing effects of, the Great Resignation.

Journaling Questions:

- Do you feel like you're burning out? Rate your current situation on a scale of 1-10.
- What do you notice about yourself that you feel could be a sign that you're about to burn out?

Now that we've covered burnout and how it could actually be a signal for change, let's explore the concept of office microcultures.

4

THE NEW CAREER MODEL: ENTER THE OFFICE MICROCULTURE

S o, if the traditional career model is becoming obsolete, what will replace it? There's a case to be made that the gig economy will continue to rise in prominence in years to come. Certainly, there will still be people who find their way in life through the traditional career model. However, as more people transition to models where they work for themselves, the traditional career model remains at risk. Therefore, the traditional career model must either be retired, or it must adapt to the new world.

Studies have shown that organizational culture can have an immense impact on a company's bottom line. In a survey of public companies, those with healthy workplace cultures were 2.5 times more likely to see significant increases in their stock price over a three-year period. Clearly, there's something to the idea that a healthy workplace sees higher productivity and value. A workplace does not need to be a cold, heartless place in order to have a high monetary value. Perhaps it's time we consider potential adaptations to the traditional career model and enact them in modern workplaces.

Therefore, I propose an extension to the idea that the traditional career model should adapt. The answer is already within reach: understanding workplace microcultures.

WHAT ARE MICROCULTURES?

Let's start off by defining what exactly a "culture" is with respect to the workplace. Typically speaking, culture refers to "the way things are done around here." It's hard to pin culture to one single-sentence definition, but it incorporates things like the people you work with, the values of those people, what those people believe in, and how those people act, particularly in relation to one another.

So, if culture broadly defined relates to the behaviors that everyone partakes in a given organization or social group, then microculture simply relates to the behaviors of smaller factions that exist within the organization at large. In other words, microculture represents the culture of a smaller group within a larger company. You might find that you enjoy learning as part of the job, or that you naturally lead your team with efficiency.

What's the Difference Between a Culture and a Microculture?

While there is no one definitive way of defining a culture vs. a microculture, you can simply think of a microculture as a distinct subset of a more general organizational culture. This is the point or level on the organizational chart where working on a team starts to feel like working for a completely separate company, because the goals you're focusing on are distinct from the ones that other teams might be working on. This could also involve nuances like differences in the technical language used and how workplaces are set up.

Finding Your Microculture

It can be hard to establish whether an organization's culture is the right fit for you from the get-go. That's because most of the aspects that make up a true culture are invisible, and it's even harder to discern with microcultures. When you're interviewing for a new job, you must present yourself as simultaneously neutral, while also being "the right fit" for not just the role, but the company culture. This is difficult to achieve when you haven't seen the inside of the company. Very often, what separates a hire from a rejection is not based on the candidate's technical skills. Rather, it's the idea of best "fit" or getting along with the group that determines who wins the job. Does the candidate have a clear idea of what those qualities are during the interview? Usually, no. We give our best effort and hope for a good outcome. But, the sting of rejection in the thanks-but-it's-not-you letter is real, and job seekers never really know why they weren't hired. Instead of fighting to get on a bus that is moving down the road, first decide whether you want to take a trip with these strangers in the first place.

Fortunately, there are some steps you can take to see inside the company's microculture before you decide whether it's right for you. Three things that you can focus on to give you a hint of what the workplace microculture is like include:

- The tools people use and how they use them
- The leaders of the group or department and how they act
- The language that's used to communicate within that culture

There are no hard and fast rules about what you should want from a microculture. This is entirely dependent on your own unique needs. However, it's good to give some thought as to what kind of culture you'd like to be a part of, refracted through those three key variables (i.e., tools, leaders, and language). Think about how you use these things in your everyday life, and how they might work within the company.

WHY WORK CULTURE MATTERS

Before we dive into microcultures, let's take a moment to think about work culture in general. If your work culture is positive, you'll attract talent and engagement, and it will impact the team dynamic, which contributes to job satisfaction. Every business has its own personality. The brand personality is designed by the marketing team, influenced by trends and marketing research, and is then spread across advertising and social media channels. Within the context of the workplace, the work culture is completely different and is influenced by a variety of factors. Workplace culture is impacted by everything including management, company policies, the type of people we work with, and the leadership within teams.

A culture is difficult to copy. As businesses strive to innovate, they face a growing problem: traditional models rapidly become obsolete. For example, the traditional career model has become obsolete because of several technological innovations over the past two decades, allowing for the emergence of the gig economy. Consequently, business environments faced a choice: maintain a competitive edge or foster a healthy culture. If the past two years have taught us anything, it's that these things do not have to be mutually exclusive. Although business must remain competitive in order to thrive, it's my opinion that fostering a healthy culture is, in and of itself, a competitive edge. Staff retention is a concern among HR professionals, and one of the reasons cited for the Great Resignation is unhealthy work environments. By fostering a healthy environment, companies hold the key to maintaining a competitive edge.

It's my observation that culture and performance correlate. Correlation does not equal causation, but according to McKinsey and Company's Organizational Health Index (based on their research of over 1,000 organizations, totaling over 3 million individuals), positive work cultures translate to up to 60% higher stock prices. A healthy work culture allows room for adaptation within its organization. As much as we enjoy getting comfy, unfortunately, the one constant in life is that change is inevitable. Businesses and organizations thrive on change. Healthy organizations respond positively to change, but unhealthy organizations resist it.

The key is this: if your workplace culture is unhealthy, your business will suffer. Maybe it will be underperformance, or in the worst-case scenario, you might even be shut down. How many headlines have you seen this past year about a corporate giant that fell because of a toxic workplace culture? An unhealthy culture leads to a loss of productivity, which leads to a fall in sales, which consequently leads to budget cutbacks, which creates an even worse culture.

Workplace cultures tend to form naturally. However, this is not the best course of action. Without a preexisting definition, or at least an idea of what we want our company culture to look like, the ramifications can be disastrous. Instead of creating the policies we want to create, we base our decisions on what other employers do. This means that our workplace isn't truly our own. This leads us to hire employees who simply don't fit within that culture, and who feel unsupported and unwanted. As a result, employee engagement suffers. This comes from dysfunctional management styles which hamper communication.

When we create a workplace based on the ideas and practices of others, it is because we lack our own vision. Without a mission, without understanding our values, we cannot create a workplace identity. The workplace becomes lackluster and draining. Our everyday actions aren't at the forefront of our decisions and this affects the formation of culture.

So, what can we, as leaders, employees, and managers, do?

Simple: step back, evaluate, and genuinely consider the type of environment you would like to cultivate. Would you like your team to feel like a little family? Perhaps you want to have a clearly defined hierarchy with well-defined boundaries. Or do you think your team would thrive in an egalitarian democracy, where everyone is heard and respected? Once you've defined the workplace culture you would like to cultivate, and you can be its architect. Make a plan and work toward it. This is the foundation of your future, so it's important to take it seriously.

You can use all kinds of tools to help build your company culture. Anonymous surveys are the most straightforward way of determining where your company culture currently sits. These reveal holes in the current culture which may need patching over, which you can direct some resources into fixing. Also, don't underestimate the power of observation. Meetings, discussions, everyday behavior, and even interviews will build a picture of your present culture. The three most important words you will ever hear about fixing your culture are: open a dialogue.

Company culture will always be a work in progress. Change is the one constant in life, and that also applies to company culture. This is why your business strategy should include adapting your company culture to the present times. Because of its importance, it needs to be a priority. This is the best way to retain staff and improve productivity. However, you might not be so sure as to what kind of culture you want. Do you want to foster learning, or a functional machine? Perhaps it's time to take a look at the concept of microcultures.

THE TYPES OF MICROCULTURES

The concept of microcultures continues to fascinate and confuse professionals. I realize that we're all sick of the pandemic, but here's the thing: there was nothing normal about it. It disrupted our lives and our workplaces, and it forever changed the way we approach work. Remote working had already been on the rise since before Covid-19 came barging in, and remote working gave us the opportunity to understand how our workplaces function. The question has gone from "Why is the company culture failing?" to "What is my company's culture?"

As I said at the start of this book, the traditional career model is in dire need of adaptation. Microcultures are unique to each workplace, although they can be categorized. I have personally identified five types that I'm sharing with you in this book. While every microculture is unique in its own way, an easy way to consider what kind of microculture best suits your individual needs is to look at the five types of microcultures that exist:

- The Classroom
- The Island
- The Swiss Watch
- The Kingdom
- The Tribe

Over the next few chapters, we'll take a closer look at each of these microcultures so you can get a better sense of what kinds of things you want to see in your ideal microculture, and what elements you want to stay away from. If there's anything we've learned from the onset and rise of remote working, it's that one size does not fit all when it comes to workplaces and work styles. This is why it's important to decide what kind of culture you want to cultivate or be a part of.

Journaling Questions:

- What does culture mean to you?
- Based on the cultures you've been a part of, what are the particular features that make you feel comfortable and at ease at work? What specific cultural aspects turn you off?

Now that we've covered what microcultures are, let's dive deeper into each type of microculture, starting with The Classroom.

5

THE STRAIGHT A'S CLASSROOM

N ina decides to become a nurse to help people. She likes babies, so she decides to work in a hospital NICU after graduating from her nursing program. She enjoys the work, loves

working with new parents, and is mentored by her older co-work-
ers. Her job responsibilities grow as she becomes more experienced,
and the hospital provides tuition reimbursement and time off for
her professional advancement. She starts taking classes toward an
advanced nursing degree.

In this example, Nina is in a Classroom microculture, where she's newly graduated and following the established path for professional development and advancement. In this chapter, we'll go over the defining characteristics of a Classroom microculture.

WHAT GOES ON IN THE CLASSROOM MICROCULTURE?

The Classroom is similar to the conventional school system. Employees are hired, trained, evaluated, and given opportunities in advance. Their bosses are professional mentors who develop talent and reward them for accomplishments. Entry-level employees are all equal and can take advantage of opportunities and grow in job title and responsibility. Managers are invested in employee development and don't hold them back due to job scarcity or jealousy.

You can see why the Classroom microculture is tied to the school system. Just like in school, as long as you follow the same structured path that's been spelled out by your teachers and the school system, you can continue to achieve preset rewards while gaining knowledge. As a result, this type of microculture is best suited to new entrants to the workforce who want to expand their skill set and grow on an established path. This includes newly graduated students or students who are close to finishing their studies and looking for internships. As people who are both young and have little professional working experience, this provides a reliable and straightforward avenue for expanding their knowledge while climbing up the professional ladder.

Who Will Thrive in the Classroom?

First and foremost, people who love learning and professional development will thrive in a Classroom microculture. Secondly, people who enjoy a well-defined structure will thrive in this microculture, and thirdly, so will people who like to know where everything is. If you're the kind of person who walks into a room and wants to know without asking where the books on managerial economics are kept, this is the microculture for you. If you're the kind of person who wants to feel safe asking what you might consider "a dumb question," this is the environment for you. An innate desire to progress is vital to succeeding in the Classroom.

You might be wondering if the Classroom is just an extension of the traditional career model. You're right; it is. It's a slightly adapted version of the traditional career model, and it doesn't rely on your job being the only thing that defines you. Being in the Classroom means there is room to grow as both a person and a professional. Under the traditional career model, you are beholden to your career, making it the sole purpose of your existence. When you're made redundant, or you decide to switch careers, you feel like the world has been pulled from under you. The beauty of the Classroom microculture is that you are continuously learning and growing your skills, which means you will be in a good position should you be made redundant or otherwise find yourself unemployed.

Who Will Struggle in the Classroom?

Dennis has known for a long time that he wants to be a lawyer. He has a passion for sports, so he decides to go into athlete representation. His undergraduate degree is in Sports Management, so when he gets to law school, he demonstrates that he's familiar with the field. His classes are focused mostly on "thinking like a lawyer" and by the time he graduates, he's excited to represent young professionals like him. When he starts an entry-level position at a small law firm, his older coworkers are happy to mentor him. As he becomes more experienced, he's assigned more cases to work on and his responsibilities grow. Soon, he starts to visit colleges and speak to young athletes about the legal aspects of professional sports. Dennis starts to become well known in his field, and his partners at the law firm are proud of his growing skills.

Although Dennis enjoys the work and is sufficiently challenged, he isn't making the changes to the industry he once dreamed of. Working with athletes and hearing about how they're taken advantage of deeply upsets him, and he wishes he was in a position of power to help. While he can advise them and be a part of the team that takes on the case, he's stuck doing the paperwork and research in his entry-level position. Dennis would like some more leadership experience but doesn't know how to get it. He begins to wonder if this firm is the right fit for him, and soon starts to question the company culture.

People who enjoy learning thrive in the Classroom. When you enter a classroom in a school, there's a structure that's clearly defined. You have the teacher at the front of the classroom, and all the desks are neatly arranged. It's a space designed for guidance, and it's a space we're all accustomed to. However, there are always one or two, or even a small group, who struggle with this structure. They prefer to explore on their own and are considered "a nuisance" or "a distraction" to the rest of the class. Translated to the example of Dennis, a Classroom microculture is a great place to learn and grow at an entry-level. At some point, this environment can become too restrictive when it's time to push boundaries and become entrepreneurial.

Unfortunately, the highly structured path means this type of microculture is not well-suited for mavericks or highly-skilled individuals who want to make big changes or possibly take over management. That's because change works against structure, and vice versa. A high degree of structure impedes change and can be stifling for creativity. Therefore, if you're someone who's interested in making big changes and disrupting the status quo, then the Classroom probably isn't a good fit for you.

When Does the Bell Ring for the Classroom?

Many people find the Classroom a great place to start their career, and learn as they grow, but what happens when there are no more lessons to learn? Eventually, the bell has to ring, class has to end, and it's time to move on to the next chapter. A Classroom environment doesn't suit everyone, and it may never suit you for the entirety of your career. That's why it's important to recognize when you've outgrown the Classroom, and when it's time to move on.

It's time to leave the Classroom when a high level of expertise in an area is achieved. The Classroom is good for learning, training, and gaining experience and/or certifications. This is also a place, like a hospital or company, that reimburses employees for school tuition. Once you have your degree (which may or may not be in the field you are working in currently), you may be able to seek an entry or mid-level management position. A lot of companies promote tuition reimbursement programs to attract young or new talent in the hopes of keeping them in the organization. If you want to stay and advance through the ranks where you are, great! If not, you have gained a lot in the time spent in the Classroom and it's time to advance elsewhere.

<u>Journaling Questions:</u>

- Do you think the Classroom microculture creates a successful business?
- What about the Classroom microculture does/does not appeal to you?

The Classroom is a great place to learn and grow as a person and a professional. Life is about the journey, not the destination, and the Classroom microculture ensures that that journey is full of lifelong lessons and plenty of opportunities for mentoring. A love of learning is vital to thriving in this microculture. If you find that you're more of a lone wolf or like to question the integrity of the structure, you might prefer a different microculture to the Classroom. Regardless, the Classroom is not just a place for the straight-A report cards. It's a place where we can feel safe enough to ask the hard questions and have fun finding out the answers.

Now that we've talked about the Classroom Microculture, let's move on to the Island microculture.

6

THE ISLAND OF INDIVIDUALS

Nina starts taking classes toward an advanced nursing degree. Her work colleagues support her desires, and they all work together to split up duties and make sure staffing needs are met, and patient care is not compromised. After she graduates, *she posts for another position in the hospital, but in a different department, cardiology, as it suits her new degree. In her new department, everyone seems to have their own particular job function and consequently works by themselves. Nina ends up performing the set of tasks and duties day in and day out. Sometimes she sees her new boss, but more often than not, she's left to her own devices to do her job and rarely speaks to her new co-workers.*

Even though Nina is in the same hospital, working in the same profession in a similar role, the microculture has changed from a Classroom to an Island, where there's very little, if any, cross-collaboration.

WHAT HAPPENS ON THE ISLAND?

The Island microculture is made up of individuals who get along, but don't wholly work together within the team. Although collaboration will be required from time to time, it's not the main theme of this microculture. Rather, the main theme is taking initiative. If there's something you want to learn, you're expected to learn it for yourself. If there's a responsibility you want to undertake, you ask for it or you simply take it on. Your managers are the leaders of the Island, everyone else is an Islander.

This microculture is an adaptation of the traditional career model, in that it allows employees a wide degree of freedom over their work. While the traditional career model implies you will be placed in a box for the rest of your life, on the Island you have mobility. If you want to change departments, you can take some advanced courses and change when you're ready. One of the drawbacks to this structure is that it's not ideal for people who thrive on collaboration. Marketing firms are typical examples of the Island microculture. Although everyone on the team is expected to be a unit, everyone has their own part of the project. Delegation is the main theme of this microculture.

Another perfect example of an Island workplace would be financial auditing. Audits are long, tiring, and draining, and require a certain level of independence. Although there are elements of the Classroom in terms of learning and mentoring, after a certain period of time you're expected to function on your own. While you aren't expected to know everything in an Island microculture, you are expected to know enough so that you can sufficiently function independent of your team.

Who Thrives on the Island?

Sarah enjoys working independently. Although she's perfectly capable of working in a group environment, she just never seemed to "click" with it. She would much rather be doing her own thing, her own task, which contributes to a greater project. Sarah enjoys numbers, and that's why she chose to work in an accounting firm. She works on reviewing client financial statements, physical product and material inventories, and reviews record-keeping procedures. Although she's working as part of a larger audit team, she is responsible for completing her own piece of the project however she likes as long as her work is completed on time.

Given the independent nature of the Island-style workplace, people who like working by themselves are more likely to enjoy this type of workplace.

This is typically a suitable work environment for highly skilled introverts, people who are in the latter stages of their careers, entrepreneurs, and creative thinkers who need time and space to solve problems. In essence, the island is for individuals who work best on their own rather than with others.

Who Gets Voted off the Island?

- *Although Sarah enjoys being an independently functioning part of a team, she wishes she could get to know the people in her company a bit more. Outside of staff meetings, there's painfully little talking. As Sarah grows older, she starts to realize that she would like more connections in her life, and she could probably be getting that within a different work environment. Working in a team where everyone collaborates and supports each other might just be the change she needs, and she begins interviewing with other firms in search of a "warmer" atmosphere.*

Because of the self-guided nature of this work, this type of microculture is typically a bad match for entry-level workers with high social needs or anyone who enjoys extensive communication and collaboration as part of their creative process. In this microculture, it's perfectly alright to enjoy learning, but you need to be an independent learner. A certain level of autonomy is required on the Island. While you will be within a team, you will never fully be part of the team. If you're not someone who's accustomed to being alone for extended periods of time, you will literally find yourself stuck and isolated.

When to Vote Yourself off the Island

It can be lonely on the Island, and you may long for more collaboration or peer relationships. This is a natural progression in a career as we change as individuals. We may be drawn toward or away from independence based on our stages of life or career. Working parents may appreciate the island of "work from home" because it allows them flexibility to care for children or ill family members without compromising their ability to produce an income. Conversely, an employee approaching retirement, an empty-nester, or single or widowed employee may feel like they want to move off of the work island and join a workgroup for the social setting.

It would be ideal, just like in life, to have a home base where we spend most of our time, and an island getaway that we could escape to when we need a break. Much like special projects at work, "Island-style" projects may present themselves in the course of a career that can allow a short-term vacation from the routine.

Journaling Questions:

- Did you ever work with someone who belonged in the "Island" microculture?
- Do you prefer working by yourself or with others? Why?

In an Island workplace, all the individuals are formally assigned to a team, but the employee's level of expertise allows them to work independently, without any supervision or input from others. They can engage, but their work does not require it. They can set their own work pace and are not wholly dependent upon others to get their job done. These can be small business owners or "specialists" within a large company.

Now that we've covered the Island microculture, let's look at the next type of microculture: The Swiss Watch.

7

THE SWISS WATCH

A *fter a while in the cardiology department, Nina decides to apply for a position in the Labor and Delivery department*

of the same hospital. After securing her new position, she joins a team of long-serving nurses, each of whom has been working in the same department for at least seven years. The nurse she is replacing previously held the position for over 14 years. Since she's new to the job, Nina is a little slower than the others and makes mistakes here and there, which causes major interruptions in the department's overall workflow. However, her co-workers are there to support her and help her get used to her new job duties and responsibilities. Her supervisors are also helpful whenever she asks questions, and everyone works together to make the department a success.

Now Nina has switched departments a second time, moving from an Island microculture to a Swiss Watch microculture. You can notice some similarities between the Island and the Swiss Watch, in that team members are still fairly indepen-dent. However, with this Swiss Watch microculture, there's a greater need for teamwork and mutual support.

HOW "THE SWISS WATCH" WORKS

The Swiss Watch microculture is exactly what it sounds like: a well-oiled and meticulously calibrated machine that is designed to literally run like clockwork. You will have the usual structure of command, including higher and lower-level managers, and the various teams of employees. However, duties are delegated to each team, and each team is made up of a group of people whose skills rely upon each other. When the Swiss Watch fails, it fails because someone made a catastrophic mistake, or because someone didn't do their job properly. That being said, the Swiss Watch has the best protocols for when someone is sick or calls in and can't make it. Although short notice for these things isn't ideal, the Swiss Watch can handle it better than most. Film crews are a perfect example of this because so many changes on set. Location changes the day before shooting, extras cancel, contracts are still being negotiated. It's a lot to consider, and everything must run smoothly in order to function.

This is an experienced, technical, or long-term workgroup that is equal in skill and importance. Teamwork is critical to accomplishing the job, and everyone must do their part for the job to get done. People in this environment can work independently but rely upon the group. Any glitch in the system causes a breakdown in the process. A supervisor in this group can troubleshoot and support employees when needed but does not have to interfere or interject with the group often. Their best work is done when left alone, and they know it. Job skill is high, experience is high, and team-work is essential.

You can think of this as any type of workgroup or project where different tasks are highly specialized and accordingly assigned to individuals with the necessary skills. Each person's job function is unique, meaning for the most part that no one person can be replaced by another. You are truly a "cog" in the machine, albeit a well-trained and fully inde-pendent cog who is exceptional at the job you perform.

Who Fits in the Swiss Watch?

This type of microculture works best for people who are independent, competent, and self-plateaued workers. Depending on the work environment, you might refer to these individuals as "lifers," or people who have done their jobs for a long time and consequently are the best at what they do and extremely reliable. These are also people who have no intention of climbing up any further on the professional ladder and are quite content with where they are now and what they're doing.

Who Doesn't Work in the Swiss Watch?

James is a musician. Although he often worked independently for most of his career, when he works with an orchestra, it's a different story. Due to the nature of music, every instrumentalist has a role to play in bringing the music to life. James is fortunate enough to be competent with different instruments, playing violin, viola, and classical acoustic guitar, so he is usually able to find steady work. He performs beautifully and is well-liked by his director and peers, but he hesitates to commit to the group for the long term. James decides that orchestra work isn't a "forever-job," but it pays the bills well enough. His commitments to the orchestra take up a lot of time and leave little time for his own writing and performing so, he's decided that he wants to pursue something where his independence will be more of a benefit than a hindrance to his career.

Because of the highly specialized nature of working in a Swiss Watch microculture, this environment is poorly suited for anyone who wants a certain degree of flexibility or job variety in their work. Also, this is not an ideal workplace for individuals who are looking to climb the ranks quickly or move into management, as the success of the team is largely dependent on the abilities of each individual rather than the management's talent. You could say that management takes a back seat in the Swiss Watch. Although managers do keep things running, it cannot be said that they are the most important members of the team. The Swiss Watch microculture could easily be applied to science and technology careers, where everyone else's success depends on everyone else.

When Is It Time to Switch off the Swiss Watch?

This is a group of equals who do their jobs in an efficient manner and like to be a part of a team that gets a complex job done. This is not for you if one or more of your coworkers try to usurp authority or become a de facto leader. You do not need to be excessively micromanaged, upstaged, or interfered with. If a coworker or group of coworkers are trying to assert themselves over you, and upper management is not recognizing or redirecting this behavior, it is time to seek another environment. If you feel that you're being marginalized even though your work is just as critical to the end results as others, this may be happening. A clock is a beautifully balanced and precise piece of equipment and needs to be balanced to function. So does microculture. Unfortunately, some can't just leave it alone! You've heard the expression, "If it ain't broke, don't fix it!" The saying applies here. Unfortunately, you may have interlopers trying to upset the peaceful balance. Be patient and observe whether temporary disruptions become permanent, and start looking elsewhere if you need to.

Journaling Questions:

- Do you enjoy highly technical and specialized work? Or do you prefer jobs with more variety?
- Imagine what it would be like to spend a day working in a Swiss Watch microculture (or think back to a similar environment you've worked in). What do you imagine the people to be like? What are their personalities like? Would you be able to get along with them?

So far, we've covered the Classroom, The Island, and The Swiss Watch microcultures. Now we'll move on to the fourth type of microculture—The Kingdom.

8

THE KEYS TO THE KINGDOM

Having gained a decent amount of experience now in various departments, Nina is looking to move to yet another position in a different part of the hospital: the ER. She becomes the new senior nurse for the department.

Her new boss is demanding, unpleasant, and autocratic. Her coworkers are unfriendly and unwilling to pitch in if a need arises. She overhears two nurses whispering that Nina was given the job *that someone else in the department wanted and deserved. Hearing this, Nina doubles her efforts to do a good job and prove that she deserves the position. After six months of working overtime and being isolated and treated poorly by her coworkers, Nina feels burned out and wonders if the nursing profession is where she wants to spend the rest of her work life. She is so upset that she is considering leaving the profession, despite her hard work and years of education.*

With this last move, Nina has transitioned from a Swiss Watch microculture to a highly competitive Kingdom micro-culture. However, she's feeling noticeably burnt out despite her best efforts.

Now she's having a hard time figuring out if the reason she's burning out has to do with her own abilities, or whether she no longer has a passion for her profession.

WHAT IT'S LIKE WORKING IN THE KINGDOM

The Kingdom relies on a clear and competitive path to success. The hierarchy is clear, and the bosses have enviable, obvious rewards: high salaries, company cars, slick offices, travel benefits, performance bonuses, and corporate "perks." They are attractive to employees and are upwardly mobile, with many opportunities for job growth. Maybe global or glamorous, there are a lot of success stories in this group. There are a lot of "politics" and social-climbing dynamics in this kind of group.

Talent is rewarded, and competitive people thrive. In the Kingdom, microculture individual achievement reigns sovereign, almost superseding the interests of the collective culture. In fact, you might say it is the ongoing competition between "teammates" to outdo others that keeps the organization running.

Who Belongs in the Kingdom?

Paula is a stockbroker and has a growing list of clients who are extremely happy with her investment strategies and ability to achieve results. Paula initially got along well with her fellow brokers and thought she had developed solid relationships with her peers when they were training together as "newbies." Paula understood that there was some degree of performance pressure in this industry; she grew up playing sports. She knew what competition was like. Although she didn't become a professional athlete, Paula knew how to play by the rules and was never willing to undermine her teammates. The cutthroat nature of the financial services industry was still something of a shock for her, however. Marketing events and social networking functions were fraught with competition over gaining contacts, stealing clients, and "trash-talking" other brokers. The path to success in her company was clear – commissions and the size of customer accounts were the driving factors. Paula was willing to work hard to achieve an edge over her peers, but it cost her cordial relationships with her co-workers. Although she remains friendly and supportive on the soccer field, she cannot afford to act that way in the office.

Because of the highly competitive nature of The Kingdom microculture, this type of environment is a perfect fit for people who are mavericks, risk-takers, creative, career-focused, not afraid of conflict, aggressive, entrepreneurial, and aspire for C-suite level/leadership positions. If I had to give it a pop culture parallel, think of it as the *Game of Thrones* of the working world. While you won't quite "die" for your career as a contender for the Iron Throne, this is an environment where competition is highly encouraged. People will elbow you out of the way and throw you out of the window in order to get what they want.

Essentially, anyone whose primary ambitions relate in some way to world domination will find success within The Kingdom.

Who Doesn't Belong in the Kingdom?

Conversely, people who are risk-averse and looking for stability and consistency probably won't fit in in this type of environment. They will be shocked to discover just how quickly their secrets or goals will be used against them. If you're someone who values the interests of the group over your own individual interests, you likely will not enjoy working in this microculture. While the Kingdom still relies on teamwork, the common value that unites everyone is their shared ambition of outperforming the person next to them.

Office outings and drinks are common bonding experiences in any company. If you want to progress, you have to know the right people, and you have to show that you're willing to serve the Kingdom to the best of your ability. However, that doesn't always mean that the best person for the job is the person who gets it. Someone who's more qualified and more experienced, a better fit for the role, might not be promoted as they deserve. On the other hand, someone who barely fits the bill but attends all company outings and knows all the right higher-ups will almost certainly climb the ladder. Those seeking fairness and equal recognition for their work will not thrive within the Kingdom.

When Is It Time to Find a New Kingdom?

As Kingdom living can be fun, prestigious, and lucrative, the cultural stress can also take a toll. If you've been on a long ride of ups and downs and feel like you've made it to the top of the mountain, you may not have anything else to prove in this environment. Similarly, you may decide that getting to the top is not worth the time and political maneuvering it will take. The "time to leave" signals can take one of two avenues in a Kingdom—you are burnt out, or you are bored. Can you be a little bit of both? Yes!

Again, this reflects your growth and development as an individual and an employee. I decided after 13 years in a Kingdom-style career, I was overworked and stressed by the politics of my position. I had gained a wide variety of skills that gave me the ability to do my job well, so my routine became somewhat predictable. I could successfully handle situations that seasoned managers become adept at, and perhaps I was a little bored of the routine. The political challenge, however, was that I was not "in the room" when decisions about my future and my performance were being made. For highly skilled and successful individuals, the lack of self-determination becomes a major source of dissatisfaction. At some point, players in the Kingdom either become executive-level leaders, support staff, or frustrated mid-level managers, or they take an entirely different path. They start their own businesses, become consultants in their field, or retire from the Kingdom completely and spend their time on a hobby that makes them happy.

Journaling Questions:

- What are your thoughts on The Kingdom microculture? Is this environment "glamorized" in movies, books, and social media?
- Have you ever worked in or heard of a company where this type of highly competitive microculture existed? How did you feel about the environment (or how do you imagine you would have felt working in that environment)?

Now that you've seen the first four types of microcultures, let's talk about the last type of microculture: The Tribe.

9

THE TRIBE

A fter another three months as the senior nurse in the ER, Nina decides enough is enough and chooses to find a new position in an entirely new setting. She gets a job at a smaller hospital with a much smaller, albeit close-knit team. Because of the size of the team, almost everyone must know how to do the same tasks as everyone else. The upside is that everyone looks out for everyone else's interests, and she can count on her co-workers to be *there for her whenever she needs their help. In fact, the group is so close that they often hang out after work together. Nina no longer feels the burnout she felt in her previous role and has found a renewed passion for the nursing profession.*

Finally, Nina has moved from the Kingdom microculture that caused her to doubt her own abilities and life goals to a more welcoming Tribe microculture, where she felt she could fit in more naturally.

WHAT IT'S LIKE WORKING IN THE TRIBE

The Tribe is exactly what it sounds like—a close-knit group. Employees in this setting enjoy cohesiveness and cooperation. All agree on the mission, purpose, and how to perform the job. They all do the same type of job and work in a production-style setting. Employee values and behaviors are all the same—harmonious. Relationships are so good that workgroups often socialize outside of work and may engage in company-sponsored sports teams or charitable events. No one seeks to rise above or outpace another. This workgroup is settled and happy and will go where directed together. If you listen closely, you may even hear them singing "Kumbaya" around a crackling campfire.

I always tell people that when companies say, "We're like a little family," it's a red flag. Usually, it's a tactic to draw you in with promises of a nice environment which ends up feeling like a toxic situation. In the case of the Tribe, the family dynamic is actually true. The Tribe functions like a family, albeit one where everyone isn't related by blood. Managers feel more like parental or guardian figures; employees feel like cousins, aunts, or siblings in some very close cases. Work spouses and work siblings are common in this microculture. Everyone has their own in-jokes, they have their own shorthand for almost everything, and some coworkers have their own slang. Productivity tends to be much higher within the Tribe because everyone enjoys coming in and has the energy to do their job.

Who Belongs to the Tribe?

Jordan grew up in a close-knit family. Church every Sunday followed by a massive family feast, a cousin was getting married every month, and every year there was a huge pile of Christmas cards to send and presents to receive. It's no surprise that when he found his first job, working as an office assistant, he learned everybody's names and brought leftovers every Monday to share with them. While this was a surprise to his coworkers at first, with some of them thinking he was playing some kind of game, it soon became apparent that this was just who he was, and it spread throughout the office. Friendships were formed, and jokes were made, and when Jordan's last day came, it was like everybody was sending their son off to college. The team had become a Tribe.

The high level of cohesion in this type of microculture makes it a good option for those who have high social needs, are friendly, and believe that their peers are just as important as work tasks. In other words, these are people who treat their co-workers as family and expect to be treated as such in their work environment. To a certain degree, you might say that the people who work well in Tribe microcultures show up to work largely to spend time with their family rather than trying to climb any sort of ladder toward success.

Who Doesn't Belong in the Tribe?

On the other hand, the highly social nature of the Tribe microculture means it's not as fitting for people who tend to diverge from group beliefs or aspire to be leaders. The Tribe already has a set hierarchy, and while there is career mobility, it's not as cutthroat as the Kingdom. You cannot barge past with your elbows and knees and expect everyone to respect you because of your harshly-earned title in the Tribe. In this microculture, everything is earned through merit. You earn respect through the courtesy you show others, and everyone is treated as an equal.

There are disadvantages to the Tribe, of course. The social nature of the Tribe also means that introverts are not as likely to enjoy working in this type of environment. While introverts can be quite social, they might find the Tribe dynamic too open and noisy for them to feel like they belong. Working in a team where everyone gets along and is encouraged to talk can, for a new person, feel quite exhausting if they aren't inclined to regular socializing. While company bar nights and events aren't mandatory to attend, if you don't like being pressured to attend these events, you won't thrive within this microculture, so seek an environment like the Classroom or the Swiss Watch.

When Is it Time to Leave the Tribe?

When you belong to the Tribe, leaving may be hard because the relationship with co-workers is so fulfilling. But if your level of expertise and experience is one where you can advance or attain a well-paying position elsewhere, it may be time to leave. People who leave and miss their coworkers or leave and ask to come back to their old jobs have experienced the challenges of losing the 'place they belong.' The most comfortable transition is to leave the Tribe for another one that has the added benefits you desire.

You may also consider leaving a Tribe microculture if you are not fully accepted in the group. It can feel very cold and isolating to not be included in the lunches and extracurricular invites to happy hour that is so common in this microculture. If you are not a fit, you feel it painfully, and there is no sense in trying to force the relationships. Sure, there is an initial time period where you have to make an effort to get to know your coworkers and get along, but if you find yourself constantly trying to seek approval that never comes or feels "genuine," it's time to move on and preserve your efforts for your actual work, not your coworkers.

Journaling Questions:

- Does Tribe microculture create the best work environment? Is a Tribe the best microculture to have in business?
- Have you been on the "inside" or the "outside" of this type of group? How does it feel to be included and excluded in this type of microculture?

Now that we've reviewed all five types of microcultures, let's go over how you can figure out which type of microculture you're walking into on your next job, so you don't get caught off guard like Nina.

10

HOW TO IDENTIFY A MICROCULTURE

As you can see from the previous chapters, even the slightest difference in a microculture can have a huge impact on your individual wellbeing. However, in Nina's case, she could possibly have saved herself the trouble of stepping into cultures where she didn't feel she belonged. In this chapter, we'll explore why it's important to identify an employer's microculture early on, and how you can go about getting an idea of what it's like to work for a potential employer.

WHY IT'S IMPORTANT TO IDENTIFY THE MICROCULTURE

Nina's story isn't as far-fetched or exaggerated as you might think. If the recent trend in resignations sweeping the world is any indication, millions of people are fed up with their work. Over half of survey respondents from a study conducted by Indeed reported experiencing burnout in 2021. The study compared year-over-year data, and one of the most notable factors in the increase of burnout was the Covid-19 pandemic. While some people simply enjoyed freedom from the office, others found that they were reflecting on the office culture and how it affected them.

According to the Indeed study, there is a slight generational divide. While Millennials and Generation Z reported similar levels of burnout, 59%, and 58%, respectively, Baby Boomers report a lower rate of burnout. Overall, 80% of workers believe that the pandemic and working from home impacted workplace burnout. 67% of those respondents believed that burnout worsened as a result, although the minority 13% believe that working from home improved their burnout. It's interesting to bring up the working from home versus working on-site debate. Approximately 38% say that working from home made burnout worse, compared to 28% who said it made burnout easier to cope with. Then there are the outliers: 25% of on-site workers said that the pandemic didn't change their burnout, versus 13% who said the same about working remotely.

What this indicates is that workers generally struggle to achieve the long-sought-after work-life balance. Working from home may have allowed some employees to achieve this, while others found they couldn't separate work from home. The Indeed study found this latter case to be true, with 27% of respondents reporting that they were "unable to unplug from work." Some reasons include the inability to take time off, lack of clear work/home boundaries, various stress factors, and financial concerns. Worker type and generational differences also come into consideration. Gen Z, Gen X, and Baby Boomers all reported that paying bills was a top concern, while 40% of Millennials were stressed by the lack of free time or PTO.

While there are many causes for burnout, one of the biggest factors, as we've mentioned, is the degree of fit between an individual and the workplace culture. If the microculture you're walking into does not fit well with your personal preferences and needs, it can have a strong negative impact on how engaged you feel on the job, your job satisfaction, and your overall job performance.

How to Pick Up on a Potential Employer's Microculture

You will never really know what the microculture of a particular company's division or team looks and feels like. However, there are still some steps you can take during the interview process to help give you a better sense of what it would be like to work there. Here are some questions you can ask your interviewer to give you some insight into their microculture:

On How the Company Engages with Employees

What makes you proud to work with your team?

This will give you a good taste of the interpersonal dynamics within the company. A Tribal response might be, "Our group cohesion is incredible; everyone supports each other and is on hand to help if anyone needs it." If you're looking for a Classroom microculture, you should keep an ear out for how knowledge is shared within the team, and how the team supports each other in searching for new opportunities. Asking this question gives you a good idea of what's expected of you in the event of a job offer, and how you're expected to fit within the team.

How do the organization and your team support your professional development?

This is one for those seeking the Classroom, the Kingdom, or the Swiss Watch. Within all three of these microcultures, there will most certainly be opportunities for professional development, but they will be offered in different ways. The Classroom will listen to the professional development track you want to take. A ground-level office manager might want to transition into HR, and a Classroom microculture will assist them with the appropriate training courses. Meanwhile, the Kingdom will offer it to those who they feel deserve it most. Betty might have produced the highest quality in the services the company offers, but Tom is a shark when it comes to drawing in new clients, so he gets the career-defining training seminar. In the Swiss Watch, due to the highly specialized nature of the team, you are offered professional development in relation to your role. If you work as a sound engineer for an audio production company, you might find that your professional development requires learning new machines and recording software.

Is risk-taking encouraged here? What happens when people fail or make mistakes?

Risk-taking, to a lesser or greater degree, is encouraged in most jobs. More so in the Kingdom and the Classroom than the Tribe, the Swiss Watch, and the Island. A Kingdom microculture will be enthusiastic and excited to hear that you're a risk-taker, while the Classroom will be happy to help you succeed in your professional development. On the other hand, because the Island is individualistic, all risk-taking is taken upon yourself. Within the Tribe, all risks are taken as a team. You fail and learn together, and you cele-brate successes together. Taking a risk in the Swiss Watch means that you're risking the entire dynamic falling flat on its face in the event of failure.

What role do team values play in the hiring process and perfor-mance reviews?

The bottom line is this: the hiring process is there to make sure you're the best fit possible for the team. By asking for team values, you can also decide if the company is the right fit for you. A company that values determination, risk-taking, and a desire to eventually be the best at what they do is a company looking for a new member of the Kingdom. A company that values togetherness and teamwork would like to open the Tribe to a new member. The Classroom wants people who desire to learn and grow, the Swiss Watch wants someone who is organized and can slot right in, and the Island wants someone who can work with a high degree of independence.

What's one thing you wish you could change about your team's dynamics?

This will tell you what you need to know about how the company views team dynamics and productivity. A hiring manager who regrets that the team "spends too much time talking" is a manager who wishes that their team would be a little bit more concerned about quarterly numbers than whose birthday it is. However, a hiring manager who "wishes that people talked more" is a hiring manager who wishes that their team got along and could connect more outside of company functions.

On How the Team Deals with Office Politics

What causes conflict? How does it get resolved?

"Office politics" is everything from personality clashes to the weird standoffs that take place at the photocopier. In general, it's advisable to let the manager handle conflicts.

However, this will vary depending on the microculture we're dealing with. The Kingdom is a dog-eat-dog environment where office politics play out like an episode of *Game of Thrones*, only with less death, so it's every man for himself. The Tribe will use more harmonious tactics, while the Classroom will be more by-the-book. I want to say that the Swiss Watch doesn't suffer from this problem, and the same with the Island, but the truth is that office politics affect everyone. The Swiss Watch is very swift with reprimands, and the Island will usually leave employees to handle it themselves.

How would you describe the "office politics" in your department?

"Office politics" is the social structure of the workplace. When asking this question, you want to keep an ear out for metaphors that will give you an idea of the microculture you're looking to enter. Anything to do with hierarchy will indicate a Kingdom, for example.

What happens when there's a disagreement over a high-stakes decision?

The Kingdom will surely remove the perceived "weaker party" in the event of a disagreement. While this might not mean someone is fired, it certainly will mean that that person will be out of sight for a while, perhaps on the ground floor while the higher-ups are making the decisions. The Tribe and the Classroom will be more civilized, offering the opportunity to talk it out and resolve any disagreements. The Swiss Watch has no time for disagreements, and the

Island will let people work it out for themselves. High-stakes decisions happen regularly within the workplace, and it's difficult to avoid them. That's why it's important to know early on how a company handles these things.

How do people like to give and receive feedback?

Everybody loves an ego boost. However, feedback is not always an ego boost. It could be constructive criticism, or it could be a flat-out crushing of the soul. That latter example is common in the Kingdom, and it's a huge part of why I left that environment. The Tribe will feel like a consistent ego boost, with criticism being more constructive than crushing. A Classroom environment will feel like your teacher is grading you while you sit there. Meanwhile, the Island will focus on your degree of independence. Feedback on the Island is so individualized that it can be a personal growth experience more than professional development. You will find criticism in the Swiss Watch revolves around your performance rather than your role in the team dynamic.

Forgetting the titles, who on the team has the power to make things happen?

It's difficult to "forget titles" within the Kingdom and the Swiss Watch. The Kingdom is so reliant on titles and hierarchy that forgetting who's in charge is detrimental to the entire structure. Meanwhile, the Swiss Watch is a power unto itself. Forgetting titles in this microculture will not lead to a disaster, but everyone here has the power to make things happen because everyone is specialized and trained according to their role. The Classroom will offer a more traditional route, such as leaving it in the hands of managers, while the Island will leave it up to the individuals to make things happen. In the Tribe, everyone supports each other, and everyone agrees on the important decisions which need to be made.

On Day-To-Day Work

How does your team celebrate success?

Successes happen every day, whether that's being offered the job, or the team reaching a huge quarterly goal. You want to succeed in your career, and you want to be a part of the team's success. Some companies, particularly those with a Kingdom or Island dynamic, will dole out quarterly or monthly bonuses as an egalitarian measure of success. In the Tribe, you might be subject to a few hugs here and there, with some high fives and a group night out. Success in the Classroom is celebrated by having your name and achievement listed in the monthly newsletter, while the Island allows people to celebrate their success as they see fit. The Swiss Watch will also celebrate together, but not to the same extent as the Tribe.

How do you support and motivate your team as a manager?

Managers have tough jobs. I should know, I was one for a long time, and I now run my own company. However, each manager has their own style. You may have heard the "carrot and stick" approach. The carrot is the reward. The stick is the punishment. Managers in the Kingdom often use this tactic, tempting you with a delicious carrot reward, but beating you with the stick of disappointment when you make a mistake. The Classroom will offer multiple attempts for you to get up and try again, with the carrot being the lessons learned along the way. In the Tribe, everyone shares the carrot and the stick, while the Islanders each get their own carrots and use their own sticks as they please. Within the Swiss Watch, there are more sticks than carrots to go around, but the carrots are bigger and richer, and the sticks are often smaller. You want to know what kind of carrot you can expect, and what sort of stick to brace yourself for.

Does the organization offer any flexible work arrangements?

This question is less to do with microcultures, and more to do with how companies have adapted over the past two years. It's not unreasonable to ask about flexible working arrangements after a global event where remote working was suddenly an option. Additionally, you need to understand how much time you'll be expected to commit to work, and how this will affect your personal life as well. You might find that the Kingdom, which you would expect to offer no flexible working arrangements, will offer some generous options. Meanwhile, the Tribe might have no flexible arrangements at all. This is why it's less to do with the microculture, and more to do with the company and type of role being filled.

What kind of social events do you attend outside of work?

The Kingdom will offer networking events, while the Tribe will focus on more social outings. Networking events will offer the chance to meet people "you should know" and rub elbows with the company's elite. It gets your face seen and your name known. A Tribe is literally like a family going out for brunch or drinks after a family gathering, so expect mention of corporate lunches at high-end restaurants. Meanwhile, the Swiss Watch and Island might not have such events. They may have an annual get-together to celebrate major holidays, but don't expect much in the way of bonding time. When you're in a Classroom environment, management doesn't tend to mix with employees unless there's a requirement. Typically, everyone will be on a corporate learning retreat.

How does someone in this role work best with everyone else on the team?

Finally, you want to know how you'll be expected to fit in. After all, regardless of the microculture, you will be expected to be "the right fit." That's why you're being interviewed. In the Tribe, you want to be seen as part of the family, welcomed almost like a long-lost cousin. However, in places with an Island dynamic, you want to be able to slot right in and just start working. Everyone is so independent on the Island of Individuals that nobody will notice you. The Swiss Watch tells a similar story, but you also have to be able to communicate clearly from the beginning, lest the machine malfunction. The Classroom will expect you to start knowing nothing, excited to learn the team dynamic and find your own place. However, you will notice that someone who is looking for a new member of the Kingdom wants someone who's eager to find their place at the top of the hierarchy.

While asking these questions may seem like overkill, it's important that you make sure that you can actually see yourself working in this new work environment before you accept the job offer

If you go into a new job blindly, you run the risk of working a job that you might not like, not necessarily because of the work itself but because of everything else related to the job— i.e., the work environment. Doing your homework early on in the interview process can save you lots of emotional and physical stress related to burnout, not to mention the hassle of eventually having to find a new job.

Journaling Questions:

- What are some questions you might ask in your next interview to give you a better picture of the employer's microculture?
- Write down at least five things you'd look for in the microculture of a new job. Now order them starting with the most important.

Now that we've gone through some ways you can get a feel for a team's microculture before you accept a job offer, we'll provide some additional resources in the next chapter to help you in the event that you do start to suffer from burnout or become overly stressed from work.

11

WHICH MICROCULTURE FITS BEST?

We've covered the five microcultures, and the failings of the traditional career model, and we now understand burnout a little bit better. With all this in mind, it's time to ask ourselves a very important question: "Which microculture suits ME best?" As of right now, you might feel on the outskirts of the Kingdom, when actually you're best suited to another environment. In this day and age, with the onset of the Great Resignation, it's more important than ever that we understand where we belong.

Do not settle for a "tolerable" work environment. If you're currently in your "survival job" (a job that people take up because it pays the bills), you might get settled and feel tempted to stay because it's easy. However, settling into a survival job can often mean allowing yourself to feel isolated in a microculture that doesn't fit you. While I understand the temptation, it's vital that you do not allow this to happen.

A good work environment is like growing a garden—start small, tend it, observe, and nurture it, so it grows into something that is healthy and productive. This takes time, attention, and investment in yourself and your best work style. Learn your preferences and how you work best and strive to be in a great place. This is the key to making a career that is enjoyable and worthwhile, not just a job to pay the bills.

There's a saying which has made its way through various forms of media: "Life is about the journey, not the destination." Well, I would like to amend that to suit the workplace: a career is a journey, not a destination. It can seem like the destination while you're training for it, but ultimately you will start out like anyone else at the very beginning. It's like taking a trip or planning a vacation. Do you want to stop along the way at gas stations and eat junk food, or travel down the road to a cozy restaurant with homemade dinners?

How you "travel" and where you "stay" on the vacation that is your career is just as important as the destination. Make sure it's a good trip! Just like you don't abandon a once-in-a-lifetime trip to Hawaii because you don't like the long lines at the airport, don't give up on a career because the current job is making you miserable. Travel in style, and invest in the best environment available!

THE NEXT STEP

The most important step is always the next one. For you, that might mean leaving your job. For another person, it might mean playing the long game and getting ready for a new career while working their current job. Even if you are not currently planning to leave a job, knowing what a great place looks like can help you spot an opportunity or refine what you want in the future. While it's okay and sometimes absolutely necessary to work in a job because it's a "right now" thing, don't give up on the overall path and don't think that you are trapped forever. If you intend on something better, you will find it.

Finding Your Fit

You are the one in control. Although it might seem like there's a higher power or other force at play, or that your manager has a hold over your life, that will never be the case. When we're new to the world of work, we are the ones who have to prove that we fit in. As we mature and gain more experience, we realize that our workplace also needs to suit us. When starting out in a career, Classroom or Tribe micro-cultures may be the best way to grow in skills while being mentored as a part of the job. It's much easier to work in a learning environment with many steps and opportunities for feedback than trying to seek out and convince a mentor to take you under their wing.

Microcultures within a job that partner formalized on-the-job training and skill enrichment courses are excellent ways to comfortably gain expertise that you can leverage into advancement opportunities. Once established in a career with a valuable skill set, the options for choosing a microculture expand. This is best seen in the "Island"—a valuable employee can be left alone to work as they choose with minimal supervision.

This is also characteristic of a Swiss Watch—all employees in the group have a recognized level of expertise and understand the mechanics of their position. They can be "left in peace" to do their work with minimal interference because they have the experience and "cred" to be left alone if they so choose. This is best suited for mature workers—and I don't mean age. We're talking about a level of professionalism that is attained either by education, experience, or talent. This microculture is all about respect for your abilities and it is shown in your ability to "self-determine."

The Kingdom can come along in your career any time you want to capture it. Make your mark, shoot to the top like a comet, and "fight" for your ideas. If you like motivating groups of people for a cause, identifying and developing new markets, or just taking a product, group, or business line and 'running with it,' this is the place for you! Truthfully, we need you in the business world. Your belief in the "mission" is what motivates people to get out of bed and join you on the ride. Striving feels a lot like 'living' in an otherwise dull and routine world. Kingdom style groups have a clear purpose, are willing to take risks, and winning is a reward like no other.

If you're a leader on a mission, you will be celebrated for your successes and have "followers" to help you along the way. Kingdom groups have their own shared compass and feel best when they feel like they are striving and achieving new exciting goals. You belong in a Kingdom if you feel restless and bored. Like Vikings that need a raid, you need a path, goal, and a mission. Being idle is not good for you, and to feel productive, seek out new projects, or volunteer for goal-driven teams in the workplace.

12

THE EVOLUTION OF YOUR ROLE IN A MICROCULTURE

Just because you take breaks doesn't mean you're broken.

— CURTIS TYRONE JONES

Technical skills change and develop over the course of a career, as well as the type of skills needed. People skills should also develop as we gain more experience, and what was once tolerable may now become abrasive in a workgroup. It is logical that our fit within a microculture can change over time as we grow and develop. A microculture is not forever; it is as dynamic as you are as an employee and individual.

It is important not to blame yourself for not recognizing unhealthy work patterns earlier on. Recognizing them now is a sign that you are growing as a person. As you evolve, your understanding does as well. Change is hard for a lot of people—wanting security is natural and the basis of living a stable, healthy life. You may not want to change jobs or leave a company or career for many good reasons, and as long as the work environment is not toxic or detrimental to your physical and mental health, you don't have to.

Becoming a mentor to other members within a microculture creates full-circle satisfaction at any stage of a career. As new people join a department or team, there is value in sharing what you know or helping orient others.

Doing different jobs within a workgroup can also help develop your skills and provide new challenges in a safe way. Diversifying yourself or taking other jobs within a company can be a way of changing your microculture to suit your growth and evolution. Networking with other employees outside of your workgroup can be beneficial. Having the "inside scoop" on job opportunities can give you a path for transfer as well.

Sometimes, despite your efforts to fit in, network, and get along, you will still encounter a few less-desirable elements in the workplace.

13

BAD APPLES IN EVERY BARREL

Every workplace will have its drama. That's a fact of working life. You will not get along with every person you meet; that's impossible. However, you can be civil and respectful. Personality clashes are more common than you would expect, but there are ways around them. Let's have a quick word about human nature and the inevitability of difficult personalities and conflict in workgroups and further validation of the workplace struggle.

No discussion of workplaces is valid if the presence of "difficult" people is not identified. It is rare to find a group filled entirely with mature, professional, and emotionally healthy individuals. Difficult coworkers are in every microculture. Any successful strategy to sidestep the co-worker landmines will work in all microcultures. Regardless, do not engage in unproductive behavior at work! Your time and career are too valuable to get distracted by anything that does not serve your highest purpose.

HOW TO AVOID BAD APPLES

It's easier than you think to fall into the barrel of bad apples, and you may find yourself surrounded by them. In my experience working for a Fortune 100 company, I can tell you that it's a slippery slope. The slippery slope fallacy implies that a small action can have significant consequences. While this certainly can be the case, it's a fallacy because it's often used to suggest the worst-case scenario. I use it to exemplify how things can happen without you noticing. When I was working as an Operations Manager, I enjoyed the job. I did not enjoy the work environment. One of the reasons I became so burned out was how little energy I was spending on the actual job, and how much I was spending listening to idle and vindictive gossip and trying to put out endless fires that had nothing to do with our products – it was all "people."

You might find that your coworkers are gossiping about people they barely know because they have nothing else to focus on. However, this will foster a negative work environment. Below are a few things to look out for in order to recognize when you might be affected by the bad apple mentality.

Disparaging team members, regardless of how badly they behave - wastes YOUR time

Although it can be cathartic to vent about that one particular coworker you don't get along with, it's only a waste of time and energy. You might think that your coworkers vent "once in a while," but actually, it's more like "once an hour" or "once a day." Listening to that complaining is just as exhausting as the actual conflict and only fosters a negative environment. Instead, tune out and spend that time and energy focusing on work, and making yourself stand out. The chances are that management already knows about the venting. Management will deal with your coworkers and whatever issue they're causing, and they might also associate you with the problem. It takes more than one person to create a hostile atmosphere: the one causing trouble and the person (or people) responding to it.

Let managers manage their problems, and you focus on your best work

There are managers and employees for a reason. Managers are there to manage the day-to-day running of the business, and employees are there to handle the base tasks. It's under-standable that you might feel more responsible if you've been in your role a long time. Employees often take on managerial duties for some positions but are not themselves managers. Some employees find themselves taking on these responsibilities in an effort to go "above and beyond," but instead become exhausted and overworked. If this is the case for you, please remember that you are not the manager. Focus on doing your job to the best of your ability.

Don't criticize your project or product - suggest improvements to the process, not people, if it's needed

If there's one thing that screams "I don't want to be here" and is a one-way ticket to being fired, it's criticizing your project or product. Or even the company itself. People don't want to work with someone who's overly critical of every little thing. Instead of complaining that the project is below your pay grade, or you aren't skilled enough to do it, suggest a way to make it more challenging. Ask your manager for something that you feel is worth your energy.

Avoid creating/participating in cliques at work - this isolates you from the greater purpose and muddies your "brand" as an intelligent and capable employee

I feel that this needs to be said: the workplace is not the cafeteria in *Mean Girls*. There are no Jocks, Nerds, or Plastics. Instead, there are employees, and managers. Creating cliques, and participating in them, only serves to undermine your brand and image. The people who create these cliques want to exert power or control over others. If you want people to see you as a hard worker who enjoys their job, it's best not to divide yourself from the rest of the workplace. This is also a waste of your time and energy. Instead of working and cultivating a nice workspace for yourself, you are actively participating in tearing it apart.

Make goals for yourself outside of work. You're bigger than the job - remembering that won't make you feel trapped

I know it feels this way now, but work is not life. It's not the only thing in your life that matters. Yes, keep your job to pay the bills, but it's perfectly fine to have hobbies outside of work. You might have taken acting classes as a teenager and have always wanted to return to it as an adult. While you work, there's nothing stopping you from signing up for an acting class or taking part in amateur theater. You are allowed to have your own interests and hobbies outside of work, and you are allowed to have personal goals as well as professional.

Here's the deal: no one is perfect all the time, but if you "audit" yourself once in a while, you can make adjustments that will keep you on track. Watch out for the clique behavior in particular, and avoid letting work take over your life. Life is about more than paying bills and dying. You are allowed to live the life that best fulfills you. Here are some things you can do which will help enrich your workplace:

Recognize that coworkers are all at different stages of development in their lives and careers

You might have worked for your company for one year, five years, or ten years. There's always going to be someone who started last week, or last month, or even today. Of course, they aren't going to be as familiar with the job as you are.

Instead of criticizing them for their slowness or unwillingness to get along, try recognizing where they are. You might have just started your job a few weeks ago and are feeling burned out by the expectations placed upon you. Here's the thing: you're new! You aren't supposed to be the best at your job yet. Speak to a manager about anyone who is making you feel like you don't belong there.

It's easy to think of where someone should be but knowing where they are is more valuable. Think of how you felt when you were new, when people were acting like you should have been perfect from the beginning. This probably contributed to your eventual burnout. They might need more training, and they might feel nervous and unable to work with people they just met. It's important to make them feel welcome and supported as they start a very scary stage of their career.

We all have lessons to learn, so while it is necessary to expect professional conduct, understand that for some it is a struggle that they will never master

There's a fine balance to be achieved in workplace relationships. You might have a "work spouse" or someone who's like a mysteriously rich aunt who enjoys their wine. There's always a level of professional conduct that needs to be achieved. Some people will never master it. They might be the happy, relaxed person who enjoys making people laugh, but they're contrasted by working under a cold boss who doesn't appreciate their conduct. This goes back to what I said before, about recognizing that life is more than your job.

Boundaries between managers and employees, and team members, must be clearly drawn at all times. Set firm boundaries with anyone who disrespects your time, ideas or personal space.

Some cohesive workgroups, like the Tribe, can evolve like this, and there's nothing wrong with you if you feel like you don't fit anymore

People grow, and sometimes they feel they've outgrown their current role. It happens, and you don't need to be overly concerned about it. When a plant outgrows its current vessel, it needs to be transferred to something larger. Otherwise, it will begin to wither and die. True, you are not a plant, but the metaphor holds true. Once you outgrow a role, it's only natural that you would desire seeking greener pastures. That could mean leaving for an altogether new role, or it could mean moving up within the company.

<u>Journaling Questions:</u>

- Have you been affected in your career by bad apples without realizing it?
- How can you make your workplace healthier?
- Do you feel you've outgrown your present role?

Now that we've covered negativity, and how to spot the signs and make the workplace healthier, it's time to address the elephant in the room: knowing when it's time to leave.

14

HOW DO I KNOW IT'S TIME TO LEAVE?

This is possibly the hardest question you will ever have to ask yourself in your professional life. You might not always know the answer, but the answer will always present itself sooner or later. When you've spent a long time working with people you've gotten to know, it can be a difficult decision in a job you know so well. If there's one thing I would like you to take away from this book, it's that there's more to life than going to college and landing the one job you'll do for the rest of your life. None of us could have predicted the 2020 pandemic, and none of us will be able to predict what will happen next year. We can make plans around it, sure, but life doesn't always follow a plan. With this in mind, there are ways you can tell if it's time for you to seek greener pastures.

SIGNS IT'S TIME TO LEAVE

Below are a few signs that it's time to leave your current job and seek something new. You might relate to all of these, or only some. You don't have to leave your job right away, but you can start exploring your options, and understand what's most important to you while you search.

The Sunday Night Blues

The first, and most obvious, sign that it's time to move on are the "Sunday night blues." It's that feeling of abject misery that crops up on a Sunday night as you dread going into work tomorrow. No job should leave you feeling such a deep sense of dread that you don't want to go in. It's easy enough to say "I'll go in, do what I have to do, then leave," but the workday slog can drag on by, and as time goes on it will only get worse. This can spiral into depression, and an even deeper sense of not belonging.

The Environment Has Become Toxic

I'm not talking about climate change; I'm talking about your work environment. Although it's not always obvious where the toxicity lies, the feeling is always the same: tension, walking on eggshells, trying to navigate a tricky situation; every conversation feels like a test you didn't prepare for. Toxic situations at work can be avoided, and even stopped, but it can be difficult to keep the peace without it affecting you. A toxic workplace can leave you feeling emotionally and mentally drained, which leads to stress, which also causes severe burnout. Recognizing a toxic situation might tell you that it's time to leave.

You're No Longer Growing

When you're no longer growing in your current company, you have two options: seek new opportunities for growth in the form of a new job, or seek opportunities for growth at your current job. Often, you will find that you've grown as far as you can within your current role and it's no longer serving you. Your manager might keep you on the hook with promises of growth "in the future," but the future could be a long time. In that time, you could have achieved a lot in the way of personal and professional growth. Don't miss out on opportunities just because you're comfortable where you are.

You're Hardly Working, Not Working Hard

Okay, that pun was awful, but the point remains: if you find you're procrastinating more than you're working, it might be time to leave. When you go to work, you're being paid to do a job, and if you aren't doing that job, you run the risk of being let go or facing disciplinary action. Procrastination doesn't happen because we're lazy. It happens because we're bored or unstimulated. We need new challenges, paired with appropriate rest, in order to thrive and keep learning and working to the best of our ability. If you're no longer working, it's time to leave.

Your Health Is Suffering

In addition to your mental health, your physical health will suffer too. Stress can inhibit your immune system, leaving you more susceptible to diseases like the flu and gastrointestinal disorders. We covered addiction in chapter 3 when we looked at burnout, and this is another thing to consider when it comes to your health. When we become addicted to things, we try to justify to ourselves why it's actually alright we're doing these things. "I smoke a pack a day, and I feel like I could run a marathon" might be the case in your 20s, but in your 30s, it might be starkly different. We do the same with alcohol, "It's only one drink," but that one drink might be every day, and it might extend to two or three drinks a day. The rationalizations continue, and they will pile up and take a toll on your health. Your health is your wealth, and it's well worth taking care of. If your job is taking a toll on your health, it's time to leave.

The Dark Triad

The psychologists among you might be familiar with the Dark Triad. Narcissism, Machiavellianism, and psychopathy. They are typically referred to as "dark" because they're considered negative personality traits. Narcissistic managers will always find a way to make you feel like the weakest member of the team, even if you are one of the strongest and most valuable. Additionally, they might steal your ideas and gaslight you into believing you had nothing to do with them, showing Machiavellian tendencies. This means that they don't care how they achieve a goal; they will achieve it at all costs. Finally, a psychopathic manager will not care about what you have going on in your personal life; they will force you to make work your life. If you see any or all of these qualities in your managers, it's time to leave.

Unfortunately, the dark triad lends itself to a charismatic style of leadership. Employees are motivated to higher levels of performance by these leaders who offer inspiring visions. Ironically, this can be threatening to the mental health of employees, especially if the charismatic manager in question possesses all three dark traits. According to psychologists, the "personalized need for power, negative life themes, and narcissistic tendencies of personalized charismatic leaders can lead to unethical and destructive behavior" (Fragouli, 2018). The dark triad lends a sense of confidence which boosts the charisma of the leader in question. As a result, the employees they inspire come to view them as heroes or embodiments of honor. This can be quite damaging to relationships of all kinds, resulting in a less than desirable workplace.

THE LEAVING PROCESS

If you decide to leave a position (or are asked to leave) it is important to do so with dignity and clarity. Do this for yourself and your company. You might be tempted to throw a tantrum and get upset, and it's your right to be upset, but word travels. Your former employer might contact your current employer and tell them about the way you left. It's also important for the people you work with or *used* to work with, that you leave with dignity and decorum. Think of it like this:

Not all relationships in work or life last forever. It's not meant to be that way! You might have one or two friends whom you've known since elementary school, or perhaps you've remained in contact with friends from old workplaces. Not everyone has that. We all have acquaintances on Facebook or other social media platforms, and we all see snippets of each other's lives through that medium. But that's just what they are, snippets. We aren't meant to be in each other's lives forever; we're meant to keep moving forward, and that ultimately means that some relationships get left behind.

Sometimes, we can't understand a situation without perspective and space. For this reason, it's important to take the time to give this to yourself. Look at your contract, or into your company's policies, and see if it's possible for you to take a career break, or a sabbatical. Most companies will have a sabbatical policy. A sabbatical can be up to one year, unpaid, for you to pursue other things. That could be teaching abroad, pursuing a creative goal, or seeking further education or training. Or even just some time off to get space from the work environment which is taking a toll on your health.

If work makes you feel sick, unappreciated, or unfulfilled, it's time to leave. You can hand in your notice or seek a new job, or you could take a sabbatical and get some space. However you decide to pursue leaving, that's up to you. There is more important work for you to do in this world and this is the wake-up call that something else needs your time and attention.

Set some absolutes for yourself and your job. These are lines that, if crossed, prompt you to begin the exit process. If you find yourself rationalizing, justifying, or explaining bad behavior to yourself or others, stop making excuses. This is a red flag and it won't go away. So save your time and sanity. Examples:

- If your company/leadership is committing crimes or violations of any governmental or professional codes
- If your leaders or managers exhibit characteristics of the Dark Triad (and this is more common than not), start looking elsewhere even if you are not yet in the line of fire
- If your ideas are stolen and you do not receive credit or reward
- You do the bulk of your job and someone else's and your plate is getting fuller
- Attempts to offer productive solutions to job processes or organization are met with scorn, indifference, or are dismissed as not important

- If you are harassed, bullied, mocked, or feel unsafe in any way
- Management is unwilling, incompetent, or incapable of recognizing and correcting major problems in the workplace

Journaling Questions:

- How do you feel when you wake up on a Monday morning?
- Do you work or procrastinate when you're at work?
- Do you have clear boundaries in place that, when broken, signal that it's time for you to begin the exit process?

Burnout is difficult to treat. If you go to your doctor or psychiatrist, you might be prescribed regular physical activity, a good night's sleep or, in more extreme cases, medication. Many of my clients come to me with work-related back issues, and Chiropractic is wonderful for the body, but I can't follow my patients home and heal their souls. In the next section, we're going to look at some ways of dealing with burnout.

15

HELPFUL TIPS AND RESOURCES
FOR STRESS MANAGEMENT

The unfortunate thing about stress is that you can't always escape it. At some point in your life, stress will find its way into your day and possibly ruin your mood. But you don't have to let it take control. Here are some resources and tools you can use to help pull yourself out of stress mode.

THE TYPES OF STRESS

There are four kinds of stress: acute stress, episodic acute stress, chronic stress, and eustress.

Acute stress is a short-term reaction to an external stressor. This could be a positive stressor or a negative stressor. Acute stress is the most common type of stress, that you will come across in your day-to-day life. It's the stress we feel when we get good news (a positive stressor) or when we accidentally send an off-color text message to the wrong person (a negative stressor). Acute stress lasts anywhere from a couple of seconds to a couple of hours, and it will start to dissipate once the stressor has been resolved. This could be allowing the good news to settle in or clearing the air with the person you accidentally texted, to resolve those two examples.

Episodic acute stress is stress which feels like it has become a way of life. When stress occurs so frequently that you learn to live with it, you are experiencing episodic acute stress. You might feel as if you'll never have a moment of peace or relaxation again, or as if they're few and far between. Some people say that it's the result of multiple episodes of acute stress, hence the name "episodic acute stress," but it can be one long period of stress as well. You might experience episodic acute stress if you're the employee who continually takes on new responsibilities, always signs up for different projects, and is always busy.

Chronic stress occurs when the pressure doesn't let up. Like the overgrown plant in the plant pot, you want to burst out and throw your soil everywhere... but you can't because you feel trapped. Chronic stress is most commonly associated with bad relationships, but it can occur in bad jobs, and this is the kind of stress which leads to burnout. It's the state of being so stressed all the time that it takes up all your energy. You know you're experiencing chronic stress when there seems to be no end in sight, unless the key stressor is removed completely, or dealt with.

It may surprise you to learn, but **eustress** is a positive kind of stress. It's often mistaken for an adrenaline rush. You might experience a sudden influx of positive emotions, happiness, excitement, ecstasy, and even love, when you encounter a positive stressor. Being promoted at work, or even opening up an email with a new job offer are both examples of positive stressors which lead to periods of this beautiful, positive type of stress. This is a fun, exciting type of stress which can trigger a feeling of euphoria.

The Stress Cycle

When we get stressed, the body responds with the stress cycle. The short version is that you experience a stressor, which releases a combination of hormones, including cortisol and adrenaline, which leads to physical symptoms. These symptoms can include anything, such as increased heart rate, profuse sweating, hyperventilation, headaches, stomach aches, muscle cramps, muscle spasms, dry mouth, inability to stop talking, inability to relax, and irritability. The stress cycle is perfectly normal, but we live in a world where stress is normalized, and that's a problem. In order to understand how best to break the cycle, I'm going to give you a brief summary of how it actually happens.

1. You experience an **external stressor**. Maybe it's because Becky at work used the last paper cone at the water cooler, maybe the photocopier isn't working again, or maybe you forgot your headphones and now have to listen to gym music as you workout. It doesn't matter what the external stressor is; it will lead to the second stage of the stress cycle.

2. Before, during, or after the external stressor, you will experience **internal appraisal**. At this point, your senses are working overtime to get information to your amygdala, the part of your brain responsible for emotional processing. It's your amygdala that tells your body that something is wrong, and it gets the hypothalamus and pituitary gland involved. Your body is a fan of homeostasis, balance, and it's these two parts of the brain that help maintain it. It's the hypothalamus and pituitary gland which bring us to stage three.

3. The **physiological response** is how you know you're stressed, though you probably ignore it. Now that the amygdala, hypothalamus, and pituitary gland are all active, your sympathetic nervous system sets to "fight or flight" mode. Your heartbeat picks up as your cardiovascular system is stimulated. You breathe heavier, get a headache, and a lot of things happen in your body, one of which is that your parasympathetic nervous system will become

suppressed. Injury and illness are now more likely to occur, and you will begin to experience gastrointestinal distress as the stomach and intestines slow down. Stage four comes next.

4. When **internalization** occurs, it's because we are aware that we're stressed. Physical reactions are more noticeable. You might feel your heartbeat a lot more, and become painfully aware of your breathing. It's at this point that you will begin to experience other symptoms such as anxiety, insomnia, and even depression. Ironically, these things could end up making you even more stressed, and then it's time to move on to stage five.

5. You can start the **coping** stage by admitting that you're stressed and doing something about it. Find your coping mechanisms and put them to action. Take a bubble bath, do some yoga, go to the gym and squat your stress away. Be careful, though: these strategies can easily become a way to avoid your problems. Set a time limit on how long you exercise. I advise looking for coping strategies which deviate from your current responsibilities. For example, if you have to stare at a computer screen for hours on end at work, it might not be the best idea to spend hours at night playing video games. Find a coping mechanism that gets you away from your computer and into your own space.

Ideas for Stress Management

There are many things you can do to help get rid of the cloud of stress you feel looming above you. Many of these might feel tired or over-recommended. There's a reason for that: they work. The trick is letting them work and not expecting it to be instant. When I attended my first yoga class and cooked my first healthy meal, I was disappointed that I didn't feel better immediately. Once it became habitual to include yoga practice three times a week and cut back on my sugar and caffeine, I began to feel better over time. Of course, this is entirely my own experience.

It may also surprise you to learn that there's scientific backing to many of the ideas I'm about to throw your way. While you deal with the cause of your stress, you can begin to take care of your symptoms. This will help you build some solid groundwork for the next phase in your life and career.

Try some of these out:

Research shows that **engaging in physical activity** can reduce stress levels. A 2014 study suggests that people who regularly exercise "are more resistant to the emotional effects of acute stress, which in turn, may protect them against diseases related to chronic stress burden" (Childs and de Wit, 2014). Physical activity offers us a chance to step away from our stressors and focus on our own goals. Exercise is a chance to celebrate what your body can do, going for a walk is a chance to get in touch with nature, and doing chores is a chance to give yourself a peaceful space. "Physical activity" doesn't have to mean weightlifting or running a half marathon every night. You could simply start an herb garden and get some movement in while tending to your plants.

Another way to improve your stress is to **eat healthy**. No, I don't mean go vegan or cut out all of your favorite foods. I mean, make more mindful choices about what you put into your body. Take coffee, for example. I still enjoy a morning coffee with a splash of milk a few times a week, but I stick to herbal tea or infusions the rest of the time. The average office worker drinks over 1000 cups of coffee per year, averaging out at 3.1 cups per day (National Coffee Association, 2020). That's about 120 mg of caffeine a day. While the FDA considers 400mg a safe amount, this is still a lot of caffeine over the course of a year. Caffeine is a stimulant that acts on the adrenal glands. It increases brain activity, but it also increases activity in your nervous system, putting you into a state of "fight or flight." Some people are hypersensitive to caffeine, which can give them heart palpitations and migraines. Try cutting back on your caffeine intake, and see how you feel after a few weeks.

Another method you could try is to **clamp down on unhealthy habits**. You might need to enlist the aid of a therapist in this, but it's important to spot your unhealthy habits. These could be anything, including hanging out with people who don't celebrate you; regularly putting yourself in dangerous situations; using substances to dull the pain of stress; sleeping in too much; being passive-aggressive to your friends; smoking ten packs of cigarettes a day. The list goes on. Your unhealthy coping mechanisms might be helping you in the short term, but in the long term, they will cause you even more stress and potentially harm you.

If you want to calm your mind and get out of your head, **try meditating**. Meditation is the act of being in the moment, focusing on your breathing, and reminding yourself to be kind to your mind. It's an important part of yoga practice. Taking a few minutes each day to focus on your breathing can be a huge stress reliever. A simple breathing exercise you can try is to inhale until your lungs are completely filled, then sigh out heavily, as though you're pushing out all of the negative emotions and thoughts. You might feel the stress melting away, and you'll notice that your shoulders no longer feel so tense.

To add some more joy into your life, **watch comedies or partake in activities that make you laugh**. I love a good rom-com and a good buddy comedy every so often. Comedy doesn't have to be highbrow or deeply intellectual to make you laugh. One study, on the use of laughter therapy states that "laughter therapy helps reduce unpleasant feelings such as tension, anxiety, hatred, and anger, alleviates feelings of depression, and aids better interpersonal relationships" (Yim, 2016).

Humans are social creatures, and it helps to **socialize with others**. You might enjoy some alone time now and again, but when we feel lonely, we begin to notice all of our flaws and stressors even more. Getting out and being surrounded by people increases the hormones which decrease anxiety levels, allowing us to feel more confident in our ability to cope with stressors (mentalhelp.net, 2015).

Alternatively, you could **get assertive about the things you want**. This is more of an exercise in confidence than a stress management technique, although the two are related. You might find your confidence waning at work because of the way you're treated, how people respond to you, or bad management. Therefore, it stands to reason that practicing being assertive about what you want from your role will help you break out of this cycle. Don't leave it at work; take it on the road. If you're the type to always say yes and do whatever the group wants to do even though you don't like it, speak up for yourself. The word "No" is incredibly powerful, especially if you follow it up with "I would like to try something new."

You could always **give yoga a try**. I love yoga. A lot of people assume that it's just stretching, and that it's easy. That is, until they take their first yoga class. Yoga is challenging. "Yoga" is Sanskrit for "union," or "unity" depending on the translation. It's literally about the unity of mind, body, and soul. The poses, or asanas, are there to challenge you and allow you time to meditate between each transition. "The discipline of yoga offers individuals a timeless and holistic model of health and healing" (Woodyard, 2011). Although

Western medicine can do a lot of wonderful things, unfortunately, the mind is not the body. This is why it's recommended to give yoga a try, to bring your mind and body to a mutual understanding.

One way to feel less stressed is to **get more sleep**. Unfortunately, one of the worst things about being stressed is being stressed about how much sleep you know you're missing out on. Try having a "wind-down" routine where you gradually shut off all electronics and spend some time in darkness before you head to bed. Try to avoid artificial light if possible. You could also invest in a weighted blanket and some blackout curtains so that you'll find yourself cocooned in warmth and sleep-inducing dark. If you feel medical intervention is necessary, speak to your doctor and they might be able to prescribe you a sleep aid. However, do not become reliant on these, as your body will grow dependent upon, or even immune, to them.

Are your thoughts still stuck in your head? Do you need a way to get them out, but you aren't quite ready for therapy? One more option is to **start journaling**. If you don't want to start therapy, journaling is one way to get your thoughts out of your head. This will, for want of a better term, free up some space and help you feel much calmer. According to the University of Rochester, the three main benefits of journaling are:

- It can help you prioritize problems, fears, and concerns
- It helps you track any symptoms day-to-day so that you can recognize triggers and learn ways to better control them
- It provides an opportunity for positive self-talk and identifying negative thoughts and behaviors (University of Rochester, 2019)

Alternatively, **listening to relaxing music** can help you create a peaceful atmosphere. You might find heavy metal relaxing because the heavy drums and guitars are cathartic, or you might enjoy listening to some Vivaldi before bed because the music evokes nature. Research shows that listening to music that we find calming can have a significant effect on our heart rate and perceived levels of anxiety (Knight and Rickard, 2001). You might think that it doesn't work, but the next time you're on the commute to work, try sticking in your ear buds and blocking out the world with your favorite music. It can really take the stress out of rush hour!

Although it might feel awkward at first, I recommend **speaking with a counselor**. We live in a world where asking for help was, until recently, considered a weakness. As times have changed, we have become more comfortable with the idea of speaking to someone neutral. They might be able to offer advice, if you and they decide it's appropriate, but they might just listen.

You can also try out certain apps such as Headspace and Relax Now, which are smartphone apps dedicated to promoting mindfulness and emotional health.

FURTHER ADVICE

Although I have given you some advice for handling stress and stressful situations, a lot of it amounts to "Just relax" or "Get some sleep." I want to spend the next couple of pages offering some final pieces of advice which may be more practical. These changes might be difficult to put in place at first—change is always hard—but being consistent is the key. It can take up to three months to form a new habit, and once it's a habit, you will wonder how you ever got along without it.

Reduce Time on the Phone, in Front of the Computer, on Social Media

According to the UK regulator, Ofcom, the average person spends around 4.8 waking hours on their phone (BBC, 2020). In the United States, the average person spends between five to six waking hours on various mobile apps (Statista, 2021). In either case, that's almost half of your day spent scrolling on your phone. That's not including the time we spend sitting in front of computers, at the office or at home.

There's no denying that cell phones have made things much easier, from ordering coffee ahead of time to connecting with the people we love, but we also cause ourselves significant harm when we overuse them. Social media, for example, can stress us out even further when we scroll past images of our friends living ostensibly better lives than our own. Your high school friends make regular announcements, such as pregnancies, upcoming weddings, and promotions. We begin to feel that we're falling behind these people.

Scrolling through social media also uses up the brain's valuable resources which are usually dedicated to concentration and attention span. We digest still images and short form video content. This conditions the brain to digest information in short chunks of no more than a minute, so we lose concentration after a short period of time. This repeated use of social media contributes to the feeling of being burned out, according to a short survey of Bronx science students (Kulahlioglu, 2021). Part of this tech burnout is related to the excessive use of apps like Zoom and Teams during the pandemic. You might notice yourself becoming easily sidetracked and feeling less productive. This is why. Because we spend so much time on social media and our computers, aimlessly scrolling or indulging in comment fights, we lose time and end up feeling unaccomplished.

Look Within, Not Without, for What Creates Meaning in Your Career

You may have taken note of the journal prompts throughout this book. Perhaps you've read them and have decided journaling isn't for you, which is fine. However, those of you who have decided to give journaling a try need to keep something in mind: the prompts are to be answered honestly. It can be difficult to be honest with ourselves, but it's necessary for growth. Admitting that I wasn't happy in my last job took a very long time, but it was worth it in the end. Looking within and asking, "What do I really want?" is the first step to career fulfillment.

Assess your work environment when you think about meetings and interactions with coworkers in terms of the type and style of communication as well as content. Ask yourself, "Is this compatible with my style?" If the answer is "Yes," that's excellent! However, you're reading this book because you're feeling unfulfilled at work, so the chances are that the answer is "No." In this case, you need to push further and ask, "What has changed in my preferred work style?" Asking yourself open-ended questions like this will force you to be honest and develop a clearer understanding of your ideal work environment. With this new understanding, imagine the updated, ideal work environment, and search for it.

Understand That Unhappiness Is Not a Failure, It Is a Signal

This is another lesson it took me forever to learn. Happiness is up to us. The brain's job is not to keep us happy; it's to keep us alive. When we're unhappy, it's a signal that something is wrong. We are so impatient with ourselves that when something is wrong our first thought isn't, "I need to rest" or to be kind to ourselves; it's "What's wrong with me?" Being patient is such an important trait to cultivate. Failures come in all forms, but being unhappy is not one of them.

When you get a new puppy, you don't shout her into submission when she has trouble being housebroken. You're patient with her; you take your time and use encouraging words.

It's easy to be kind and supportive of others. However, when it comes to career success, we're hard on ourselves because that's how we are raised. We go to college, we get a degree, we get a job, and that's the job we do for the rest of our lives. Only now, we don't have to do it for the rest of our lives, and we feel like we've wasted a lot of time. Past experiences may not prepare you for massive career or company changes, so it's important to learn patience. These are new behaviors, and you need time and patience to make progress. Never berate yourself for getting into a "situation" or tell yourself, "I should have seen this before."

Get Outside!

You can mix this one up with being social. If the pandemic has taught us anything, it's that being locked indoors with just a computer for company isn't very fulfilling. While it was necessary, that didn't stop us from feeling lonely. Now that restrictions are being lifted, we can arrange to meet friends outdoors and indoors. We can more freely enjoy the time we spend in the sun. Getting outside and being in touch with nature are incredible stress-relieving activities. You don't need to build an expensive garden to enjoy the outdoors. Go to the park and be surrounded by the greenery. Find a botanical garden and learn about plants. Or, and this is my favorite, go stargazing! Grab a blanket and some pals, and sit under the stars, trying to name the constellations. Hard mode: turn off your phones and don't look up the names online!

As hard as it is and as weighed down as you feel, make time for physical activity and get outdoors! Sunshine and fresh air are important for Vitamin D activation—taking supplements don't help if you don't put them to work. Getting some sun-to-skin contact activates it. Running and yoga are two excellent activities to get you moving. In particular, a nice summer or warm spring run will help you feel better. You don't have to be strenuous in how you move, just consistent.

Nourish Yourself

This is something not everyone understands: the better you take care of yourself, the better you will feel. When we are young, we can eat anything they want, and it won't have any effect on sleep or performance. This changes as we age, and increased stress can accelerate shifts in metabolism and mood. Our diets can become a constant battle between what we eat, what we want, and what will make us feel good. Not everyone enjoys fruits and vegetables for example, but they're full of necessary vitamins and minerals which the body needs to support base functions. One of these base functions is hormonal regulation, and stress can have a negative impact on how they function. Cortisol and adrenaline are hormones that can easily get out of hand and cause weight gain, lower your ability to handle stress, and contribute to exhaustion and fatigue. This is, in part, why it's so important to keep on top of your nutrition.

It's crucial to understand the role of **proper nutrition** and depletion in the burnout cycle, especially if you are tired, anxious, and having trouble falling asleep—you are depleting your body of Vitamins B and C, as well as amino acids tyrosine and 5-HTP. It is easy to find high-quality supplements that can help you rebuild your immune system and improve sleep and mood without resorting to prescription medications. Speak to a chiropractor or nutritionist about the best sources of these nutrients and/or supplementation.

Final Thoughts

If change is not an option right now, plan happy activities that you can look forward to that will take your mind off of your coworkers and work environment. Something Americans tend to avoid is taking PTO. If you have PTO, take it, and enjoy it. You have more than earned it. It doesn't mean you're any more of a hard worker than anyone else because you didn't take your PTO last year; it just means you didn't put your wellbeing first. Going through the steps of planning and arranging for vacations on long weekends gives you something else to think about when you've had enough. And when you're on vacation, you can spend the time enjoying the activities you looked forward to.

WHEN SHOULD YOU CONSULT A THERAPIST

You may have negative feelings about speaking with a therapist. But the reality is, therapy can be powerful for helping find relief from the stress you're feeling.

Here are some signs that it may be time for you to seek help from a mental health professional:

- You find it difficult to control your emotions
- You aren't as productive at work
- You're going through major changes in your sleep or eating patterns
- It's hard to build and keep strong relationships
- You've suffered a traumatic episode
- You don't enjoy the activities that you typically like to do
- You're grieving over the loss of a loved one or from a relationship that's ended
- Your physical health is suffering
- You feel the urge to improve yourself but find it hard to start
- You're coping with an addictive substance

Journaling Questions:

- After reading the list above, do you think you might benefit from therapy?
- What are five things you can do to relax whenever you start to feel stressed out?

Now that we've gone through some of the resources and methods you can use to help reduce your stress, we'll provide a recap of what we've discussed in this book.

CONCLUSION

Burnout is common in the workplace. It's a byproduct of stress, and many factors have a role in how it develops. You might be a hardworking person who regularly takes on new challenges because you always need something to work on. However, constantly taking on something new and always saying yes will turn you into a drone. Burnout can happen when your work becomes your life when your work/life balance is out of order. Another reason you might be burned out is a lack of motivation. We spend a lot of time studying and working towards "the next thing."

You might have picked up this book expecting a standard self-help book about coping with burnout. While I hope to have offered some guidance in that regard, I also hope you've learned something about company microcultures and how they function. While company culture is not the only contributing factor to burnout, it plays a huge role. I hope that you've learned how to read your company's microculture, and have thought about what environment you would like to work in. I think we can assign some blame to the rigidity of the traditional career model, and its lack of adaptation, for the Great Resignation.

The traditional career model worked for a time, but it has since become obsolete. Spending years training in a field, followed by empty promises of quick progression, takes a huge toll on the mind and body. We weren't built to pay bills and die. We were born to enjoy ourselves, and a huge part of enjoying your career comes from the culture you're working in. Microcultures are an addition, an adaptation, an addendum to the traditional career model. Picking up on subtle hints with the right questions at a job interview will tell you all you need to know about the environment you could be entering.

Asking a simple, open-ended question such as "How are successes celebrated?" offers a wealth of information. A Kingdom microculture might offer scaled bonuses based on your position, while the Tribe might organize a company-sponsored night out. The possibilities are endless with such a simple question. However, it's also important to understand what microculture you would fit into and what environment you are seeking. I thrive in an environment where collaboration is key, for example, but you might be more comfortable in an environment that encourages independence.

When It's Time to Leave

While the different microcultures have their own signs for when it's time to leave, there are a few things to look out for. If you find yourself, on Sunday night, dreading going to work the next day, it might be time to leave. If you find that your body feels like it's breaking, or you're so stressed you're getting sick more often, it might be time to consider looking for another job. If you walk into work and it feels like you've just been pricked with thorns because the environment has become toxic, it's time to start drafting your resignation.

Most importantly: if your health is suffering, it's time to leave. Yes, money is vital to existence in the modern world, but money comes and goes. I recognize the position I'm coming from when I say that, but I also know that I've been in the position of someone who works just for the money. You can always retrain in something you're passionate about; you can always seek assistance where needed. You cannot recover your health if the load gets too heavy. The money you lose now will be nothing compared to the medical bills you could be facing in the future.

The Microcultures

We saw in the various stories about the microcultures that it's possible to fit within any of them. There is no "one size fits all" approach when it comes to finding the microculture that best suits you. While workplaces are expected to adapt as time goes on and as change comes, we are also expected to adapt to the changes that occur within the workplace. You might find that the Classroom has become the Island, and you yourself have gone from thriving in the Classroom to thriving in the Swiss Watch. This is normal, and you are faced with two choices: adapt to the Island, or find a Swiss Watch. When we feel alone and apart from our coworkers, that's when we begin to get stressed.

The Classroom is a meritocracy, similar to the school system. You're hired, you're trained, and are evaluated regularly, with regular opportunities to advance. While you have bosses, they assume the role of mentors who want to see your talent develop. Your talent and accomplishments are rewarded. Most importantly, in the Classroom everyone is equal, which is why it's a meritocracy. Opportunities are given on the basis of merit, and your managers and company invest in your development. While you might feel stuck in a job like this, there are opportunities to get out of the dead end.

If you prefer a microculture where delegation is the main theme, seek the Island. The Island offers a wide degree of freedom over your work. Within this, there is also career mobility. However, this is not the environment for people who enjoy working in an environment with collaboration. Everyone works on their own, occasionally communicating with each other, on their own part of the project.

For a microculture where everyone has their place, seek the well-oiled machine of the Swiss Watch. The Swiss Watch has the usual chain of command featuring managers and employees, and has the added bonus of duties and tasks being delegated as required. Although you may not always get along with your colleagues, everyone relies upon one another to see their job completed. This microculture does have the disadvantage of falling apart if one thing is out of place. With that in mind, this is the ideal microculture for anyone who wants to be a part of something, and to progress along their chosen path.

I realize that I might have been harsh on the Kingdom because of my own experiences, but I have also seen good people thrive within it and stay true to themselves. The Kingdom is not for the faint of heart. It's a place for people who are comfortable following a clear, structured, cutthroat path to success. The hierarchy is as clear as it gets, and the rewards are there to be reaped: high salaries, company cars, offices, and countless other benefits. All of this feeds an environment where competitive people can thrive. Office politics become turning points upon which these individuals can move, allowing their own careers to benefit as a result.

Finally, for those seeking a close-knit group, the Tribe offers a collaborative environment. Everything is in universal agreement. All members of the team have a united mission, purpose, and performance. While not everyone gets along, differences are overlooked and everyone works in harmony.

Promotions are sought, but no one is better than anyone else. This is a microculture where everyone is equal, even the bosses. Everyone gets along so well that, outside of company gatherings, employees might hang out outside the office. Working in the Tribe microculture has a settled, happy feel to it in which everyone has space to thrive.

Stress and Stress Management

The stress cycle is what rules the four kinds of stress: acute stress, episodic acute stress, chronic stress, and eustress. Although eustress can be positive as it encourages us to keep learning and doing new things, the stress in general can be harmful. Chronic stress dampens the immune system, leaving us more vulnerable to disease. It can also affect our sleep schedule, causing us to lose vital rest, which could help us recover. In order to break the stress cycle, it's important to develop coping mechanisms so that stress doesn't rule us.

Stress management is a skill everybody needs to learn. You don't need to be a Zen yogi every second of the day; that's impossible. However, there are ways you can manage your stress. The most effective way is to seek therapy. In doing this, you will be able to develop strategies to cope in the future. However, if you want to try something more holistic, it's a good idea to develop healthy habits. For example, practicing yoga or cutting back on caffeine can have a positive effect on your overall health. Physical activity reduces blood pressure, which can alleviate many physical symptoms of stress.

Additionally, you might be tired of hearing "Get some sleep." Yes, sleep is a great way to alleviate stress. Unfortunately, stress can cause sleep issues such as insomnia and fitful sleep. That's why it's important to find alternative means of relieving stress. Spending less time in front of your computer or on social media will disengage you from virtual reality. Although you and the people commenting are real people, the persona we put up online is not the person we are. We spend so much time cultivating the person we are online that it takes up almost half the day. You could use this time to go outside and get some sun or look within and ask yourself what you need to be happy in your career.

You might want to consult a therapist if you are experiencing any of the items on the list mentioned in chapter 14. It's not always obvious to us when we experience them. To us, an angry outburst is perfectly reasonable because we're "allowed to be angry." Yes, we can be angry, but that doesn't mean we have the right to let it control us or to use it against others. Additionally, seeking help from a therapist is usually the best course of action as they will be able to guide you through exercises designed to help you get a hold of your stress.

Happiness and fulfillment in your career are active choices. You have to decide what you truly want from your career and go for it. That choice begins with understanding which microculture best suits you. Do you prefer working within a team with a clear hierarchy, or do you prefer a laid-back environment? Do you like to get your head down and start working straight away all through the day, or do you like to have small conversations throughout the workday? The journaling prompts I have provided are there to help you build your roadmap out of burnout. The end result of your road map is open-ended. You might decide that leaving and retraining for a new career is your best option. On the other hand, you might want to stay and work your way up the ladder into a different department. Whatever you decide to do, it must be your choice, and be for your own benefit.

THANK YOU FOR YOUR PURCHASE!

Scan the QR code below
*to receive your **FREE** Interview Checklist*
*and the **Burnout to Belonging Journal Pages** to get the most out*
of our content and begin your journey to low-stress work!

REFERENCES

Abramson, A. (2022). *Burnout and stress are everywhere.* Apa.org. https://www.apa.org/monitor/2022/01/special-burnout-stress

Cabrera, E. (n.d.). *Protean organizations reshaping work and careers to retain female talent.* Retrieved May 5, 2022, from https://core.ac.uk/download/pdf/6229842.pdf

Ceci, L. (2021, October 19). *Time spent on average on a smartphone in the U.S. 2021.* Statista. https://www.statista.com/statistics/1224510/time-spent-per-day-on-smartphone-us/

COVID-19 and Employee Burnout: Maintaining Focus, Productivity, and Engagement. (2020). https://www.eaglehill

consulting.com/wp-content/uploads/EHC-COVID-19-and-Employee-Burnout-Webinar.pdf

Dewar, C., & Doucette, R. (n.d.). *Three steps to supercharge DE&I capability building | McKinsey & Company*. Www.mckinsey.com. Retrieved May 13, 2022, from https://www.mckinsey.com/business-functions/people-and-organizational-performance/our-insights/the-organization-blog/three-steps-to-supercharge-dei-capability-building

ERC. (2019, February 1). *Workplace Culture: What it is, why it matters, and how to define it*. Yourerc.com. https://www.yourerc.com/blog/post/workplace-culture-what-it-is-why-it-matters-how-to-define-it

Fisher, J. (n.d.). *Workplace burnout survey | Deloitte US*. Deloitte United States. https://www2.deloitte.com/us/en/pages/about-deloitte/articles/burnout-survey.html

Fragouli, E. (2018, July 1). *The dark-side of charisma and charismatic leadership*. Discovery.dundee.ac.uk. https://discovery.dundee.ac.uk/en/publications/the-dark-side-of-charisma-and-charismatic-leadership

Harvard Health Publishing. (2020, July 6). *Understanding the stress response*. Harvard Health; Harvard Health. https://www.health.harvard.edu/staying-healthy/understanding-the-stress-response

Indeed Study Shows That Worker Burnout Is At Frighteningly High Levels: Here Is What You Need To Do Now. (2021, April 5). *Forbes*. https://www.forbes.com/sites/jack kelly/2021/04/05/indeed-study-shows-that-worker-burnout-is-at-frighteningly-high-levels-here-is-what-you-need-to-do-now/

Knight, W. E. J., & Rickard, N. S. (2001). Relaxing Music Prevents Stress-Induced Increases in Subjective Anxiety, Systolic Blood Pressure, and Heart Rate in Healthy Males and Females. *Journal of Music Therapy*, 4(XXXVIII). http://www.chinamusictherapy.org/file/file/doc/Relaxing%20Mu sic%20Prevents%20Stress-Induced%20Increases%20in%20Subjective%20Anxiety,%20Systolic%20Blood%20Pres sure,%20and%20Heart%20Rate%20in%20Healthy.pdf

Kulahlioglu, C. (2021, April 23). *Social media's influence on our attention spans*. The Science Survey. https://thesciencesurvey.com/editorial/2021/04/23/social-medias-influence-on-our-attention-spans/

Maslach, C., & Leiter, M. P. (2016). *Understanding the burnout experience: recent research and its implications for psychiatry*. World Psychiatry. *15*(2), 103–111. https://doi.org/10.1002/wps.20311

Mental Health America | Homepage. (n.d.). Mental Health America. Retrieved May 10, 2022, from https://www.mhana

tional.org/?objectid=C7DF951E-1372-4D20-
C88B7DC5A2AE586D

Morrison, C. (2021, May 4). *16 employee burnout statistics you can't ignore*. EveryoneSocial. https://everyonesocial.com/blog/employee-burnout-statistics/

Moss, J. (2019, December 11). *Burnout is about your workplace, not your people*. Harvard Business Review. https://hbr.org/2019/12/burnout-is-about-your-workplace-not-your-people

National Coffee Association. (2020, March 26). *NCA releases 2020 national coffee data trends, the "atlas of american coffee."* Www.ncausa.org. https://www.ncausa.org/Newsroom/NCA-releases-Atlas-of-American-Coffee

Ng, K. (2021, September 1). *How to know when it's time to quit your job – and how to do it right*. The Independent. https://www.independent.co.uk/life-style/jobs-employees-how-to-quit-b1910055.html

Organizational Health Index. (2017). McKinsey & Company. https://www.mckinsey.com/solutions/orgsolutions/overview/organizational-health-index

Socialization and Altruistic Acts as Stress Relief. (2015). Mentalhelp.net. https://www.mentalhelp.net/stress/socialization-and-altruistic-acts-as-stress-relief/

Startling Remote Work Burnout Statistics (2021) | Apollo Technical. (2021, February 10). Apollo Technical LLC. https://www.apollotechnical.com/remote-work-burnout-statistics/

Stevenson, M. (2020, January 16). *Employee burnout statistics you need to know.* HR Exchange Network. https://www.hrex changenetwork.com/employee-engagement/news/employee-burnout-statistics-you-need-to-know

Stress Cycles: What they Are and How to Break Them — Embrace Sexual Wellness. (n.d.). *Embrace Sexual Wellness.* https://www.embracesexualwellness.com/esw-blog/stresscycles

Talent Report: What Workers Want in 2012 | Net Impact. (n.d.). Netimpact.org. https://netimpact.org/research-and-publica tions/talent-report-what-workers-want-in-2012

Threlkeld, K. (2021, March 11). *Employee burnout report: COVID-19's impact and 3 strategies to curb it.* Www.indeed.com. https://www.indeed.com/lead/preventing-employee-burnout-report

University of Rochester Medical Center. (2019). *Journaling for Mental Health - Health Encyclopedia - University of Rochester Medical Center.* Rochester.edu. https://www.urmc.rochester. edu/encyclopedia/content.aspx?ContentID=4552& ContentTypeID=1

Why organizational culture matters. (n.d.). Www.hcamag.com. https://www.hcamag.com/us/specialization/corporate-well ness/why-organizational-culture-matters/211100

Wigert, B., & Agrawal, S. (2018, July 12). *Employee burnout, Part 1: The 5 main causes.* Gallup.com. https://www.gallup. com/workplace/237059/employee-burnout-part-main- causes.aspx

Woodyard, C. (2011). Exploring the therapeutic effects of yoga and its ability to increase quality of life. *International Journal of Yoga, 4*(2), 49. https://doi.org/10.4103/0973-6131. 85485

Yim, J. (2016). Therapeutic Benefits of Laughter in Mental Health: A Theoretical Review. *The Tohoku Journal of Experi- mental Medicine, 239*(3), 243–249. https://doi.org/10.1620/ tjem.239.243

www.ingramcontent.com/pod-product-compliance
Lightning Source LLC
Chambersburg PA
CBHW071151120626
46546CB00006B/2209